The
Credit
Dictionary

Published by The Credo Company — Memphis, TN

Copyright © 2010 by The Credo Company, LLC

All rights reserved.

Editor: Corey P Smith

www.coreypsmith.com

Cover Design: Felix Walker

Book Design: Essex Graphix

Library of Congress Catalog Card Number: On File

Library of Congress Control Number: On File

Printed in the United States of America

The Credo Company LLC

3238 Players Club Circle

Memphis, TN 38125

Authors Statement

The title of this book is "The Credit Dictionary", but it is much more than a dictionary. I wanted to provide the reader with a complete list of terms related to credit, insurance and banking. However, I also wanted to inform people about a secret language of success and the power of words. The key to understanding success is knowing who you are and what God has instilled in you as a spiritual being. There are many people that spend their entire life in a comatose state of mind. What I mean by this is for 23 hours of the day, they are following rules and ideas of another human being. The 24th hour is used simply to reflect on the dreams that could have been and the fears that are ever present. People are taught not to live above their means, and they never realize that they were taught in the beginning to settle for contentment. Most people have their creative side of thinking stripped from the very beginning through traditional education. One of the first things we are trained as children is to go to school five days a week, seven hours a day. You are trained not to question the information being taught. You are trained to memorize useless information for the purpose of test, which breeds a robotic society. But, you never realize all these things are the makings of an economic slave. The definition of muse is to think and the definition of amuse is to entertain. Most of us spend our time being amused by those individuals that keep us in a comatose state of mind. Whether you recognize it or not, this is done with words. Marshall McLuhan once stated, "Only the small secrets need to be protected. The big ones are kept secret by public incredulity." In order to understand the true power of words you must first understand who you are, and the vibrations your words carry. I would like to offer this poem as a motivational foundation to understanding where your success begins.

"Self"

I have to live with myself and so

I want to be fit for myself to know

I want to be able as the days go by

To always look myself in the eye

I don't want to have on some closet shelf

A lot of secrets about myself

And fool myself as I come and go

Into thinking no one else will know

The kind of man I really am

I don't want to fix myself in a sham

Here in this struggle for success and health

I want to be able to like myself

I don't want to look at the setting sun

And hate myself for the things I've done

No one knows who I am like me

I see things others may never see

I want to deserve all peoples respect

Whether rich or poor, giant or elf

I want to be able to like myself

TABLE OF CONTENTS

Introduction

Generally, when people get their own way with others, they do it with words. They virtually compel others to agree with their point of view, give them what they want, do what they ask and buy what they are selling. The seduction of words is continuous. Their enormous power lies in the meaning of the words and what they mean to the person who hears them. The words elicit emotional responses in others that manipulate their thinking and behavior.

Words create impressions, images and expectations. They build psychological connections. They influence how we think. Since thoughts determine actions, there's a power connection between the words we use and the results we get. This is most often understood by the language we speak. Think about these two words: spend and invest. Would you like for me to spend your money or invest it? Since spending implies your money is gone, you would probably say invest, but either way I have persuaded you to give me your money.

Different words evoke different feelings. Poorly chosen words can kill enthusiasm, impact self–esteem, lower expectations and hold people back. Well–chosen words can motivate, offer hope, create vision, impact thinking and alter results.

Proverb 18–21 states, "The tongue has the power of life and death, and those who love it will eat its fruit." What does that mean? It means that you will live or die by what you speak. Remember this, by saying a word with deep intention and focus, we are creating sound vibration which acts as the effective body of the words power, training the mind to view the word as important, allowing the power of that word to become part of us, and most of all Becoming That Word! Make your word become something people can believe. Learn to say what you mean and mean what you say.

Power of Words

The tongue is the most versatile part of the body. I believe the reason for this is because it's how we translate language by way of words that carry vibrations. Let me give you an example of how this works. There is a technique that many preachers use called the "voice roll." A voice roll sounds like the preacher is talking to the beat of a metronome or as though he were emphasizing every word in a pattern. The preacher will usually deliver the words like a heart rate of 45 to 60 beats per minute. For instance, he might repeat this pattern "he's worthy, he's worthy, he's worthy."

Think about the normal routine followed when you attend most churches. The choir usually sings first and the assistant pastor comes out next. He induces a "build up" process or begins to generate the excitement and the expectations of the audience. During this time someone may sing another song. Remember this, gospel songs are great for building excitement and involvement. In the middle of this entire process someone may react as, if they have the Holy Spirit. This increases the intensity in the church. At this point conversion tactics are being mixed. The result is the audience's attention span is now totally focused upon the communication, while the environment becomes more exciting or tense.

Then, the pastor comes out and talks about the devil, going to hell, the end of the world or what it takes to go to heaven. All this does is increase the tension and fear. Now, don't get me wrong, I believe in God with all my heart, but I just want people to understand the power of words and the vibrations they carry. Think about this, music is mesmerizing and it can be used as a weapon. It can make you laugh, cry, dance or turn your emotions and thoughts into actions. This is all done with the use of words mixed with instruments to create music. This is what I'm talking about, when I say preachers preach emphasizing every word in a patterned style. This leads me to mention vibrato. Vibrato is the tremulous effect imparted in some vocal or instrumental music, and the cycle-per-second-range. This causes people to go into an altered state of consciousness. This is what I mean when I say music is "Mesmerizing."

The repetition of powerful words has been a special part of most all world religions and most every mystic tradition. This process of selecting words of potency and vibrating them from the body creates waves of energy which both attune you to your goal and call forth the support of the entire universe. Whether you believe it or not words carry power because we give them meaning. Think about this, the word hate or bitch has no power, but it's how you mix those words with your emotions.

When we speak a word, a subtle yet powerful vibration is created from our bodies which carries out into the universe. These vibrations are the manifest form or body of the meaning we ascribe to the words we say. In addition, focusing the mind on that word trains the mind to believe the power of that word is important. If, the word bitch meant Queen our emotions or reactions towards its vibration when spoken would be different. The more we intone the word, the more we begin to resonate to the word and attract more of the emotions and energy it carries into our lives.

Language of Success

In Matthew 12:36–37, the bible states, "But I tell you that every careless word that people speak, they shall give an accounting for it in the day of judgement. For by your words you will be justified and by your words you will be condemned."

Now, what does that mean? Every language in this world consist of words that can be put together to create power, weakness, failure or success. Spoken words carry vibrations, but it's the language that communicates ideas that are manifested through the hands of men. The language that you speak can determine your success as well as your failures.

Since the beginning of time, the use of language has been the most powerful weapon known to man. History vividly illustrates how those in commandeer of language were not only masters in persuasion and influence, but incredibly successful. Even among the uneducated, uninitiated, and disenfranchised men and women who mastered language defied the odds and accomplished the unimaginable. Those who mastered language, whether good or bad in nature had the world at their fingertips. We see and hear this language from the Pharaohs of Egypt, to Al Capone, a man who rarely spoke a word, to Barack Obama, a man who captured American sentiments of hope in one phrase, "Yes We Can."

When we think of language mastery, we instantly refer to the mastery of spoken tongues, excellent writing skills, science and mathematics. The names that cross our minds include Cornell West,

Dr. Martin Luther King, Jr., John Grisham, Stephen King, and Tom Clancy. Others may think of preachers like T.D. Jakes, or Joel Olsteen, while some think of Johnnie Cochran. All of these people have accomplished much and are masters of language.

Fortunately, this book is not about outstanding scientific discoveries or scholastic undertakings. It is not about fluff filled writings, nor is it about mastering the use of rhetoric. This book will not discuss how to speak like Joel Olsteen or Barack Obama, or how to mimic the successes of others. However, it will serve as a dictionary to those seeking to learn terms with regards to credit and banking. I also wanted to use this book as a way to teach or make people aware of the power of language, financial vibrations and words. I want you, the reader to learn a secret language, spoken only by those who are successful and those who genuinely aspire to achieve their greatest potential. Learning this secret language will help you create your own personally designed success.

Despite your starting point in life, no special accolades will be bestowed upon a person simply because they can read and comprehend on a high level. There are many highly educated scholastic icons that have been successful at nothing, except failing and remember, even a fool has the potential to become rich. Just as knowledge alone is not enough, neither are gifts and talents. There are many who possess great gifts and talents who still fail because they cannot avoid making foolish statements and bad decisions. The language of success is more than the mastery of textbook knowledge or the possession of talents and gifts.

What is language? How is the word defined? If you research the word "language," almost every source will trace the etymological origin of the word back to the 14th century, as derived from the Anglo-French, and the tongue of Latin. The terms and phrases most often used to define "language' states: language is "a systematic means of communicating ideas or feelings by the use of conventional sounds, gestures, or marks that have understood meanings in their community." This definition is fairly straightforward. Basically, language is the vehicle we use to send messages to each other. Almost every human, whether literate or not, can make basic statements to help them get what they want. So, why are so many people unsuccessful? The answer is simple. They have never learned and mastered the language of success. The language of success is based on words. Words carry vibrations and wavelengths that are understood through the use of language. For instance, any fool can master the art of begging with words, or intimidation with words, or invoking anger with words, or simply connecting with people with words. Such being true, the words of the wise have no deeper meaning than the same words spoken by a fool, if they are not used correctly.

Do we label a seemingly prudent man "wise" based on what he says alone? The answer should be a resounding NO! Wisdom maybe expressed in words by any fool, but only a wise man can demonstrate the tenets of wisdom. Do we label a religious man or woman a "devout worshipper" simply because he or she proclaims to be devout? Or do we examine their actions for demonstration of a devout religious lifestyle? Do we call a 100–meter runner the "fastest man in the world" just because he says so? Or do we watch to see, if he wins Olympic Gold in the 100–meter dash? Do we label a man a "truth speaker" simply because he says I am speaking the truth? Or do we try his statements against the known facts and assess his tendency to speak the truth over a period of time?

Actions is the voice and tongue of success. Why can't all those who master the art of talking be successful? Why do some achieve success while others seem to be hassled and detrimentally affected by every hazard in life? The answer is simple. Talk is CHEAP. In fact, talking is absolutely FREE! Here is a small thought about the language of the successful and why talk is cheap.

This illustration is taken from the movie "Talk to Me", based on a true story. The movie is staged in the heart of the Civil Rights Movement, during the late 50's and 60's. During the movie, Ralph Waldo "Petey" Greene, who so candidly referred to himself as only a con and a thief, wanted to be a DJ with a poplar D.C. radio station. "Petey" did everything in his power to get hired as a DJ with WOL, now known as Radio One. In fact, "Petey" even hosted live protests in front of the radio station building until he got the job. Once he was hired, "Petey" was incredibly successful. He touched the entire country and is credited with saving D.C. from catastrophic riot damage after Dr. King was assassinated. Most notably, "Petey" hosted a nationally syndicated talk show, and appeared on the Johnny Carson show during a time where black people were openly discriminated against. However, before "Petey" was hired, he was given three pieces of advice by his new boss, (1) Always know more than your audience, (2) Never underestimate a man, and (3) If you talk "shit", you better back it up!

Whenever "Petey" talked bad about somebody or some event, or whatever, he not only talked enough trash to fill a landfill, but he had accredited research to support every contention he ever made. When he talked shit, he backed it up. The most counterproductive force on the road to success is the failure to do what we promise to do. The world does not set these expectations. We establish them ourselves.

The successful people are masters at setting and exceeding these expectations. Failures, however, are masters at overstating what they can do and severely under-performing without any slightly acceptable reason. Let's think about it on a basic level. How would you feel, if your friend promised you a ride to work and he or she never showed up? How could that affect your employment? Would you trust that person to come through the next time? How would you feel, if you loaned someone money and they never paid you back or even mentioned the debt? Chances are, you would be disappointed, angry, frustrated and possibly ready to write that person off for good. The failure to come through, can and will destroy your chances for success.

Look at how contracts are treated today versus 50 years ago. In the past, men and women used to shake hands on a deal, and their word was bond. Transactions were simply, "You do this, and I will do that, OK, we have a deal. Let's shake on it." Things have changed in today's world. A man's word does not have nearly as much value as a signed contract. The power of a handshake no longer binds two parties to an agreement. The truth is people don't trust each other anymore. The absence of dependability has poisoned the realm of contract negotiations forever and the failure to be dependable will stifle your ascension to success. The bottom line is, when people say they are going to do something and fail to at least try, they are talking "shit" with no intention to back it up. The same was true for Ralph Waldo "Petey" Greene. He was successful because he always said what he intended to say and it always came from the heart. Petey Greene talked shit on every show, and he always backed it up. In fact, each show ended like this, "So grab your head, and make a fist. Listen to me and remember this. I'll tell it to the hot. I'll tell it to the cold. I'll tell it to the young. I'll tell it to the old. I don't want no laughing. I don't want no crying. Most of all, I don't want no signifying. Achtt!! This is Petey Greene's Washington."

If you read this book with an open mind, it will reveal the secret language that unlocks the doors of success in a world where everyone speaks the same spoken language. The world is filled with secrets and the language of success is the most openly exposed secret available. There are secret societies, secret handshakes, and secret agendas. Unlike other secrets, the language of success can be shared. The more people you share it with, the more successful you will become. What if, I told you that all failures in life speak the same language too? You also need to learn the secret language of failures. Knowing this language will help improve your selection of friends and help you recognize the best way to handle difficult people.

What language did Abraham Lincoln, Donald Trump, Oprah Winfrey, Martin Luther King, Franklin D. Roosevelt, Henry Ford, and John D. Rockefeller speak? They all speak the English language, but what secret language do they speak? They speak the language of success. The language is spoken through the manifestation of actions. Failures can never understand the language of success, but the successful recognize it on all levels. The language is simple. We are not what we say, but what we believe, because people only act on what they believe. Belief is one of the most powerful weapons in the world. Success is the result of believing, and acting on the right principles. Accordingly, failure is the result of believing the wrong thing and acting on the wrong principles. All failures speak the language of gossip, complaining, revenge, lies, discouragement and jealousy. Learning the language of success requires you to do the opposite, believe the opposite, and act on the right principles.

The language of success, is the demonstration of truth speaking, non–judgmental approaches to dealing with others, avoiding the tendency to complain, having a forgiving heart, welcoming competition, encouraging others, being honest with yourself and always being positive. Dr. Martin Luther King said, "The measure of a man is not where he stands when things are going well, but where he stands in the face of adversity and turmoil." Those who are successful act like men and women of courage and poise under fire. They understand time is valuable, however, more important than

13

time is your word. The more you become involved in accomplishing your goals, the less free time you have and the more focused and disciplined you must become. Successful people plan their time and their day in writing, so they do not break their word. If, you find yourself living life filled with clutter and counter–productive distractions, tardiness, and inconsistency, you must do the following:

(1) Write your vision and dreams down on paper.

(2) List the steps you must take to achieve your dreams.

(3) Evaluate your life and list your hobbies, obligations, and time commitments.

(4) If, more than 50% of your time is going to areas not responsive to you fulfilling your dreams, eliminate those distractions.

The term dogmatic simply means being stubborn, inflexible, unbending, and narrow. Successful people are incredibly firm in their beliefs, but they also understand the importance of seeing the whole picture. Their ideas are not solely defined by what they know, but are expanded by their capacity to concede they know everything. Successful people are not overly dogmatic, instead they are lifetime learners. Plato said it best, "This I know–That I know nothing." Successful people are always optimistic and open minded.

■

"Debt is modern day slavery
in America. Credit is simply the
slave ship that got you there"

— Jarim P.L.

Financial Vibrations

There is a reason most poor people remain broke financially their entire lives and it's not because of bad credit. Every thought or belief that any person focuses on will manifest itself by way of vibrations and energy. Those thoughts or beliefs will affect your life greatly depending on whether or not they are positive or negative. But, believe it or not there is a blueprint for positive thinking and manifesting wealth through financial vibrations. Many people have never realized that most of their thinking when it comes to money, success and wealth has been developed through schools, politics, religion and most of all parents. All of these factors set the wavelength and blueprint towards how you will perceive money, success and wealth your entire life. The majority of the population have been brainwashed to have a poverty mindset, therefore keeping them in financial bondage their whole life simply because they have no idea how to create financial success through thoughts, words and action. There are five things that you should always consider when trying to tap into your financial vibrations.

1. Be aware of the company that you surround yourself with.
2. Make a conscious attempt to live in the best possible environments.
3. If you hate what you're doing for a living, your life depends on you transitioning to something that you love or want to do.

4. Never participate in any conversation that does not enhance your life intellectually and especially financially.

5. Always pay attention to any spiritual clues that God may reveal to you in regards to visions, dreams, and regrets when it comes to your life.

* * * * * *

"Millionaires and beggars both have the same 24 hours in a day."

"Be aware of the company that you surround yourself with consistently"

There are many clichés that can sum up how the people you hang around can affect your success. The problem is that most people truly do not consider, is success can be distracted by who you keep company with, because those people will affect your thoughts, emotions, and character. Even if, you do not believe this consider that everything is a form of energy.

Think about how you will sometimes change the way you talk, dress or even change your perception depending on your environment and who you are associated with on a daily basis. I often hear people say, "I'm grown and nobody can make me do anything that I don't want to" and that's what I call a blind analysis. The strongest vibrations and energy are invisible. Energy and vibrations can be transferred easily, that is why negative people can bring your spirits down and positive people can motivate other people. If you can understand this spiritual concept, it will prompt you to guard yourself from negative thoughts, words, and most of all people. You will not even see yourself being influenced by the vibrations of the people in your circle because like I stated, "the strongest vibrations and energy are invisible. There are seven habits that you should recognize when it comes to financial vibrations. The seven habits will let you know, if you have a poor man's mentality.

These are seven habits that broke people practice.

1. They Don't Take Risk
2. They Complain All the Time
3. They Hang Around Other Broke People
4. They Always have a Negative Prospective
5. They are Jealous
6. They Always Follow the Masses
7. They are Insecure

The reason why recognizing these poor man's vibrations are so important is because it will assist you with building a blueprint of your own when it comes to attracting success and wealth. You first must understand that vibrations are real and you must focus on attracting positivity and operating on a higher frequency than a person that you engage that has a low vibration. People who live in poverty operate on a lower vibration because they are dealing with financial instability, poverty, crime, unemployment and miseducation. If you think this is not true, imagine how you would feel living in a very upscale neighborhood as opposed to living in poverty. You probably would feel more secure, accomplished, and proud. You would feel the exact opposite living in poverty such as being depressed, insecure and unaccomplished.

* * * * * *

"Surround yourself with people that reflect who you want to be, energy is contagious"

"Make a conscious attempt to live in the best possible environments"

I have always talked about living in the best possible neighborhoods that I could afford, even when I couldn't afford it. I dreamed big enough and it forced me to create and find a way to become financially able to buy my dream home. I moved in my neighborhood on purpose because I wanted to take hold of all the positive financial vibrations and successful people that live in my neighborhood. Money is energy believe it or not and most people dismiss that reality by making cliché statements like, "money is the root of all evil" and that simply is not true. People and the spirits that possess them are the root of all evil. There are people in my neighborhood that make five, ten, twenty million dollars a year and they carry those financial and mental wavelengths with them.

Think about this, every year Experian releases its annual State of Credit Report. This is a comprehensive look at the average credit scores of consumers in cities across America. This report also highlights some underlying factors that contribute to high and low credit scores. I will simplify this report for you, it's basically a study of psychological and socioeconomic behavior as it relates to credit. But, it also provides clues to how financial vibrations are affected by where you live. In my first book 'How to Outsmart the Credit Bureaus" I talked about geographical codes. There is a reason why credit bureaus use geographical codes, and census tracts to discriminate and red line. People don't understand that there are emotional and psychological vibrations that can be manifested through credit and money. When I mentioned earlier about being aware of the company that you surround yourself with, that includes your neighbors, because you are affected by their behavior as well.

One thing that stands out more than anything in Experian's State of Credit Report is that, in cities where there are lower levels of education and lower incomes, credit scores are lower. However, poor people can combat the lack of traditional education by educating themselves financially. The more educated you are about credit and debt, the more you are able to avoid financial mistakes. Remember that unemployment and low income are married.

21

* * * * * *

"To one he gave five talents, to another two, to another one, to each according to his ability"

"If you hate what you're doing for a living, your life depends on transitioning to something that you love or want to do"

There are so many people who are content with their living situation and their employment and hate both of them at the same time. I put so much emphasis on financial vibrations because it can elevate you out of your unconscious sense of contentment. When you become content with something that you hate doing you're essentially dying a slow physical, mental and spiritual death. The reason I stated that your life depends on quitting a job that you hate is because it affects your sleep, marriage, and health. I am not saying that doing what you love will turn into dollars, but doing what you love will open up the doors to financial freedom. This is a part of figuring out your financial vibrations. In most cases it will take years to truly figure out your gifts, talents and passion. That is why patience is so important. You know that cliché' "Life Is Too Short?"

Well doing something that you hate makes it shorter. When you settle into a job just to pay your bills, life will pass you by very quickly, but your misery will seem to last forever. One of the keys to recognizing your financial vibrations is focus and risk taking. In order to do these two things, you must be able to visualize your roadmap to financial freedom. This will allow you to accept the discomfort and uncertainty that comes with risk taking, but the focus aspect will give you the mental and emotional strength to take action and build your financial foundation. This is where you learn to truly leverage credit and money to build assets and income streams.

* * * * * *

"The tongue has the power of life and death, and those who love it will eat its fruit"

"Never participate in any conversation that does not enhance your life intellectually and especially financially"

The definition of gossip is casual or unconstrained conversation or reports about other people. Anytime that you find yourself discussing other people, I can almost guarantee that it's in regards to death, unhappiness, jealousy, misfortune and most of all their lack of money. All of these words are connected to some form of negative energy. Remember that certain people release positive energy and others negative energy, but either vibration could affect you financially. Think about how you feel when you lose one hundred dollars as opposed to spending one hundred dollars. Both actions carry a different vibration. If you lose one hundred dollars, you probably are going to feel down or frustrated for a little while. But, if you spend the same one hundred dollars on something that depreciates in value you will feel happy or optimistic. The reason why is because one action makes you feel like you gained something and the other makes you feel as though you lost something.

The important thing to remember about energy is that you have the power to change it in an instance. When it comes to finding your financial vibrations, you must be prepared to gain and lose something, but remain in a positive and focused space either way. Discovering your financial vibration is going to take you on a roller coaster ride of emotions, but the important thing to remember is "Experience the Emotions" and not "Become the Emotion."

* * * * * *

*"A man's gift maketh room for him,
and bringeth him before great men"*

**"Always pay attention to any spiritual clues that
God may reveal to you in regards to visions,
dreams, and regrets when it comes to your life"**

The reason most people cannot figure out what they are supposed to be doing with their life or even where their wealth lies, is because they never pay attention to the intelligence of the universe. One of

24

the gifts that God gives all of us, is the power of intuition. Intuition is a spiritual gift that can be used to interpret signs from the universe. In order to manifest your visions and dreams, you must learn to communicate with the universe. This can be done by meditation and praying. Spiritual clues can be times when you are happy, sad, excited, jealous, anxious, confident and most of all afraid. In other words, you must learn to recognize when God is leaving you clues based on when you experience these feeling and circumstances related to them. Once you learn how to interpret and dissect these moments, your visualization vibrations will become stronger. Interpreting these moments simply means paying attention to what you were feeling before and after each situation.

Spiritual clues relating to your financial vibrations could be how you feel clocking in at work or never wanting your vacation from work to end. Both of those feelings are clues being given to you from God. We are all connected to each other and the universe that we live in, because the universe is nothing more than energy. This is the reason people can bring you down through their negative vibrations. Remember in order to interpret your spiritual clues and manifest your financial vibrations, is through meditation and visualization. This is the doorway to wealth. If you hate clocking in at work, that's a clue that there is something more for you in this life. If you are happy with your job and pay, that's a clue as well. If you have dreams of relaxing on a beach and driving a nice car, that's a clue. If you're always lazy and jealous of other people who are ambitious, that's a clue.

Human beings are nothing more than matter floating around in a universe that is spinning with positive and negative energy. You are more than a physical shell and however you vibrate positive or negative, poor or rich mentality that is what you will attract. If you are vibrating at the same energy level as a broke, pessimistic person, your wavelength will attract that same vibration. This is why you must pay attention to every spiritual clue as well as your regrets and learn to control these vibrations because they are gateways to financial freedom. Remember what you think about or feel you attract. It's not even what you want that you attract, it's what you do, say think and feel.

Section 609 Affidavit Credit Dispute Letters

INTRODUCTION

Restoring your bad credit is not a difficult job if you are ready, willing and have the patience to deal with the "delay & scare tactics" of the Credit Bureaus and provided that you have the proper step-by-step instructions and the right tools to do it with.

The **609 Affidavit Credit Dispute Letters** are the proper tools to use. Don't let the simplicity of the letters and the often called "odd-ball" instructions fool you. They work, although, the time it takes to get positive results will vary from person to person considering that sometimes it may take 3 or 4 "rounds" of sending the various letters we give you in this book, but eventually these letters will force the credit bureaus to remove the negative items that you request.

In order to understand how and why this book will enable you to get all of your negative items removed from your credit reports you need to understand a little bit about the credit reporting business and the privacy laws. There are three main Credit Reporting Agencies referred to as CRA's and/or credit bureaus. They are Equifax, Experian and TransUnion.

When you engage in a credit transaction (loan, mortgage, credit card, etc.) with a bank or any other creditor the information for each of these accounts will be reported to one or more of these CRAs (credit bureaus) by each creditor and each month each "credit item"

27

will be reported in your "credit file" which is indexed under your social security number, physical address and full name.

The Fair Credit Reporting Act was put into law prior to the electronic and computer age. Even though the credit industry has been trying to lobby Congress to re–write the law to meet current technology standards, it is important to note that the current version of the Fair Credit Reporting Act (FCRA) requires the CRAs to have physical copies in their files of documentation to support each account being reported.

It is also important to understand that the creditors report all of your credit items to the credit bureaus electronically. They don't send copies of any physical documents whatsoever to the credit bureaus. **IMPORTANT: What that means is that the credit bureaus do not review and/or verify any credit applications, signed contracts or any documents whatsoever before they report the item on your credit report.** They accept any and all credit items that a creditor sends to them electronically. They accept these credit items as "true" and correct and belonging to you.

Each month, your bank or creditor sends an "electronic file" with the details of your account to each of the CRAs (credit bureaus)

- Account number
- Date opened
- Date of last activity
- High credit
- Balance
- Payment term

- Status (borrower, co–borrower, joint)
- Historical status (as agreed, 30 days delinquent
- Amount Past Due
- Payment amount
- Customer information secured from the credit application

and the credit bureaus simply place this information into your credit file with NO VERIFICATION done as to whether the account is valid, the information is correct or whether the creditor even has the right to report the item on your credit report. One of the reasons the credit bureaus do this is because the creditors are considered their true customers, not you the consumer.

Basically, the three main credit bureaus give the creditor the benefit of the doubt that they are reporting accurate information. Why would they give the creditors the benefit of the doubt you ask?

The main answer to that question is because the creditor pays the credit bureau to report the item and the creditor also pays the credit bureaus each time they pull your credit report. The credit bureaus earn hundreds of millions of dollars a year reporting anything and everything on your credit report that a creditor provides them with.

Credit bureaus are a "for-profit" business and they get paid to put items on your credit report and they get paid when these same creditors pull your credit report. Creditors are able to charge you a higher interest rate for the more negative items that are placed on your report. The problem with this method of reporting is that ANY CREDITOR can essentially report whatever they want about you,

29

whether it is correct or not. There is a major conflict of interest going on here, don't you agree?

The Federal Government saw a big problem with this method of reporting, so they thought that they solved the problem when they passed what is known as the Fair Credit Reporting Act (FCRA). It was supposed to protect the consumer and govern the activities of Credit Reporting Agencies and regulate how they report information about you. It sounds good in theory, but read on to find out why it is not working.

If you study this Federal law and also study the case law established in various court cases pertaining to various sections of the FCRA, you will see that the FCRA requires that all Credit Reporting Agencies are supposed to **VERIFY ALL INFORMATION** received from creditors **BEFORE** this information is added to your credit file.

Proper *verification* according to established case law involves the credit bureau having copies of the original signed credit application in their files. They are required to have a copy of the credit application that you signed when you opened the credit account with the creditor in their files. They are supposed to have it in their files to show that they verified the information and account belongs to you and to show that they verified the information before they placed it on your credit report.

The truth of the matter is…the credit bureaus don't review any documents let alone keep a copy of your credit application in their files. They NEVER see any documents. They don't want to see any documents. Another reason for this is because of privacy laws when it comes to sharing your personal information. What this means, is that when you open an account with Capital One Bank they must get your permission to sell or share your personal information with any company outside of their brand. That makes it difficult for the credit bureaus to get any physical information such as a signed contract or credit agreement from a creditor, if you did not give that creditor permission to share your information with companies outside of their brand.

NOTE: For those of you who have ever attempted to read the FCRA (Fair Credit Reporting Act) to see where it states that the credit bureaus are supposed to have documents on file that verify the accuracy of every account reported in your credit file. I don't have to tell you that this federal law, like most laws coming out of our United States Congress is *"clear as mud."* They are obviously written by gifted attorneys paid by lobbyists working on behalf of the big banks and the credit reporting agencies. Our congressmen and women who sit on the committees that draft up these laws obviously don't read the laws after they are written by these attorneys to see if the law that they drafted are written the way they drafted them. The FCRA law is about as easy to read as the tax code.

To help you maneuver through the "mud" I have outlined where to look in the 86–page document called the Fair Credit Reporting Act. In fact, I have broken it down to 4 paragraphs (along with my paraphrasing of those pages) to help you understand where it says in the law that the credit bureaus are supposed to have written

31

documents in their files that verify the accuracy of the accounts it reports in your credit files. And FYI, there are also important case laws (Court Decisions) that I base my paraphrasing on.

These 4 paragraphs noted below (along with my paraphrasing) reveal why these letters work

1. Page 3: § 609. **Disclosures to consumers** [15 U.S.C. § 1681g] (a) information **on file**; sources; report recipients. Every consumer reporting agency shall, upon request, and subject to 610(a) (1) [1681h], clearly and accurately disclose to the consumer.

Paraphrase: The information in the credit bureaus files (not the creditors files), mentioned above is the information that they store in their computer base on every consumer. Then 610(a) (1) [168h] identifies the proper identification required (driver license and SS card) + a written request by the consumer. Basically, it says that if a consumer asks the correct way, in writing, and has properly identified themselves, the 3 bureaus are required to disclose to the consumer exactly what documents are stored within their computer base that were used to verify the information that is being reported on them. They refuse to show you anything because they don't have anything in their files to show you. Instead, they tell you to request these documents from the original creditor.

2. Page 37 (2) Summary of rights required to be included with agency disclosures. A consumer reporting agency shall provide to a consumer, with each written disclosure by the agency to the consumer under this section–Paraphrase: This says the same thing as above... they will disclose the information requested to the consumer.

3. Page 37 (2), (E), a statement that a consumer reporting agency is not required to remove accurate derogatory information from the file of a consumer, unless the information is outdated under section 605 or **cannot be verified**.

Paraphrase: There are 2 instances revealed in subsection (2), (E), whereby *"accurate"* derogatory information can be removed. 1.) If the information is outdated in Section 605. For example, a Bankruptcy 7 will stay on a consumer's bureau for 10 years. After the 10 years, this credit file will expire or drop off from their credit report. Collections, Charge–offs, Repossessions et al, have a file span of 7 years before falling off. 2.) The information cannot be verified. "Verification" is the focal point of the deletion process. Verification is a vague term but is defined in the terms section of this document on page 7.

4. Page 7 (2) Verification (B) of the **information in the consumer's application for the credit** or insurance, to determine that the consumer meets the specific criteria bearing on credit worthiness or insurability.

Paraphrase: This is about as clear as mud. It was obviously written by a gifted attorney. Although (B) deals with credit *and* insurance for our purposes here we are only concerned with the credit portion. (2) (B) is the CREDIT APPLICATION! If you look closely, it says that it is **the "information" in the credit application** that it uses to determine whether the consumer meets that lending guidelines.

How It Is Supposed to Work: For example, let's assume you are going to purchase a car and finance that car. When the Credit department of that car dealership fund a deal with a lender, the dealer surrenders the 2 most important funding documents: the contract + the credit application. Once the lender is satisfied with these and the necessary supporting documents, the lender funds the loan. The lender now has the responsibility of reporting this consumer's file to the 3 credit bureaus.

5. The lender is supposed to send the credit application to the 3 bureaus to properly verify that this is the correct customer. This verification piece is important. It's important because the dealership has to comply with the Patriot Act and other imposed regulations to properly verify, by securing a copy of the consumers Driver's License, that the person signing the contract + the credit application is the person that was properly identified.

Also, the lender used this credit application as proof that the consumer gave the creditor the right to pull the consumer's credit file and check on the person's job, income, residence, references and then approve the loan. **The credit application is the verification piece.**

The lender then, on a monthly basis, sends its gigantic email batch file to the 3 credit bureaus for every one of their loans. In this giant file, it contains the information on every consumer that has a loan with them. The lender sends exactly what you see printed on the credit bureau report. The sent information includes:

- Account number
- Date opened
- Date of last activity
- High credit
- Balance
- Payment term
- Status (borrower, co–borrower, joint)
- Historical status (as agreed, 30 days delinquent)
- Amount past due
- Payment amount
- Customer information secured from the credit application

The problem is ... even though the law requires the credit reporting agency to verify every account it reports on before reporting on it, the fact is the lender never, ever, ever sends the credit application to the 3 credit bureaus! No lenders ever send the credit application; therefore, the credit bureau NEVER verifies any of this information. Instead of sending the CRA a copy of the credit application to be verified, the creditor pulls the credit file of the consumer and the creditor verifies the information that the consumer puts on the credit application themselves. The verification process was done backwards.

The law requires the credit reporting agency to verify the credit information not the creditor. This being the case, **anything that is included in your credit bureau file can be removed if you request the credit reporting agencies right to report the item by forcing them to show you the proof of verification that is**

supposed to be in their files. You can effectively remove both valid negative items, as well as invalid items this way.

According to the FCRA, if a credit file is going to be reported on a consumer's report, it has to be properly verified by the **credit bureau**. Each item included in a credit report has a verification piece…but, the bureaus never have it. The FCRA states that the bureaus are the ones that have to keep this verification on file, even though the bureaus will try to tell you to go directly to the creditor and request this information instead of asking the credit bureau for the documentation.

This is not good considering the lender, an unscrupulous court employee, or a collection agency, or debt buyer, could report anything they like on your credit report in an attempt to gain leverage against you to collect on an alleged debt or to justify to you why they are charging you a higher interest rate. The **Section 609 Affidavit Credit Dispute Letters** used to dispute your negative credit items are directed towards the 3 bureaus, not the creditor.

We don't care what documents the creditor has in their files. Our stance is that according to Section 609 of the FCRA, and backed up by the various established case law, credit bureaus are required to send me a copy of the documents that they used to verify the account I a disputing. If they do not have a copy of the document(s) used to verify my account then that means that they did not verify the account and the FCRA states that they are required to delete all "unverified" items.

Why don't the credit bureaus keep files if the FCRA requires them to? Because reviewing millions and millions of paper documents and then keeping them in files on their location prior to reporting the account in your credit file would be extremely difficult and time consuming and would cost a fortune in man power to do it. So, rather than go through this great expense, they instead set up an electronic reporting system and rely on a creditor to submit documentation to you if you challenge any of the items on your report. Again, it all sounds good in theory, **BUT doing it this way does NOT comply with the current law.**

The Credit Reporting Agencies simply have chosen NOT to verify the accounts in the manner that the law was written. They have never complied with the law and have gotten away with it and their attitude is that we have managed to get the law written using confusing legalese and we have lobbyists who keep the FTC from having to provide consumer with interpretations of various clauses in the FCRA, so we are OK. Their attitude is; if there are a few people who file disputes and request proof of verification and who continue to challenge us after we use our scare tactics and delay tactics, we'll simply adhere to their requests.

No exchange of original signed application documents ever takes place between the creditor and the Credit Bureau (CRA). The CRA just reports the information provided by your creditor and falsely "assumes" that it is valid and correct simply because it is being reported to them.

And when asked to VERIFY the information–the CRA will simply send an electronic communication to the creditor asking "is this information correct" and the creditor will usually respond "yes this information is correct". Then, the CRA will send you a letter or a copy of your credit report with a notation that will say, *"We have researched the credit account. The results are: we have verified that this item belongs to you."*

The Truth is, no one at the credit bureau ever actually verifies the actual credit application or any other documentation.

How do I know that this is the way they deal with disputes? I know this because I have read the transcripts where employees for various credit bureaus have admitted under oath that this is how it is done when they testified under oath in various lawsuits pertaining to the FCRA.

Were you aware of this? If you answered no, don't feel bad. Most consumers HAVE NO IDEA that this is how credit items are verified. The Credit Reporting Agencies are in violation of Federal Law when they do this, and they know they are, but since 99.9% of consumers do not know their rights they don't do anything about it. Why should they go to all that expense when they don't have to?

Not only that, to make matters worse, the FTC (Federal Trade Commission), which is supposed to regulate the Credit Bureaus and enforce the Fair Credit Reporting Act, refuses to step in when you file a complaint with them or complain that the credit bureau refuses to send you copies of the verification.

Today, if you file a complaint with the FTC, they will send you a "form letter" that states, *"We cannot act as your lawyer or intervene in a dispute between a consumer and a credit bureau or between a consumer and a creditor, or furnisher of information. The private enforcement provisions of the FCRA permit the consumer to bring a civil lawsuit for willful noncompliance with the Act."*

They will go on to inform you that if you choose to sue a credit bureau, that the FCRA allows, you may receive actual damages and/or punitive damages up to $1,000 per occurrence for the credit bureaus *willful noncompliance* with the Act (Section 616) as well as for *negligent noncompliance* and you will be able to recover actual damages sustained by you (Section 617) and that attorney fees will be allowed for both forms of your civil action if you win the lawsuit. Even though the FTC is supposed to exist to protect the consumer and to enforce the FCRA they will tell you that they can't force the credit bureaus to comply with the law, but instead, suggest that you consult with a private attorney if you fell the credit bureau is not complying with the law.

On the surface, this is very disturbing and discouraging. Well, it is and it isn't. Let me explain. The truth of the matter is that the credit bureaus are BIG for–profit corporations that have set up their own way of doing business and have indoctrinated the masses and lobbied the various government officials into believing that they are doing everything correct beyond and above, what the law requires them to do.

Why do they get away with it? They get away with it because hardly anybody ever challenges them. But guess what, the credit bureaus back off when somebody challenges them the "right way". They don't want to get sued and have to go to trail; therefore, they very seldom force you to sue them before taking the negative items off. Not because it will cost a lot of money. They have the money and resources to drag a lawsuit through the court system for years.

They don't want to risk the publicity and have the masses find out about this, especially during the current economic crisis we are going through now. They know that if they get sued and the case goes to trial, they will lose and then there will be case law on the record that could get the attention of hordes of attorneys across the country and then their entire business model would be in jeopardy.

The good news is, if you challenge the credit bureaus "right to report" an account and show them that you know your rights, they will comply with your requests **assuming you can get your letters through to a real human being. (More on that later.)** After all, the number of people who know how to do a proper dispute based on section 609 the right way is far between, so when they receive a valid dispute based on section 609, they quietly comply.

It's not a big deal to them, considering you are a grain of sand on the beach. As long as you serve them with a valid dispute in writing and you don't give up after receiving their "standard delay or intimidation reply" that they have verified the item as being valid, you will be one in a million. So, you are no threat to their business model so they will quietly remove the items that you request them to.

Valid Negative Credit Items vs. Invalid Items

The credit bureaus propaganda machine has indoctrinated the masses into believing that it is impossible to get accurate credit items removed from your credit report. But the truth of the matter is, that is false. As we discussed earlier, the law is as clear as mud. But, **"Page 37 (2), (E), a statement that a consumer reporting agency is not required to remove accurate derogatory information from the file of a consumer, unless the information is outdated under section 605, or cannot be verified."** This clause in the FCRA clearly states that they are required to remove accurate information if it cannot be verified. Most people falsely believe there is NO HOPE in removing "valid" derogatory information from their credit report and essentially give up. But nothing could be further from the truth.

Under the FCRA, Credit Reporting Agencies (Credit Bureaus) must provide a copy of the verifiable original creditor documentation if it is requested properly by you, the consumer. Since they cannot provide proof of verification to you in the form of a physical contract document per your written request to do so – the account is classified as **"UNVERIFIED"** and under the FCRA – **all UNVERIFIED accounts MUST BE DELETED**. Whether the account is correct or not–makes no difference. If the CRA cannot provide you physical verification of the account–it is an UNVERIFIED account and MUST BE DELETED.

Keep in mind the time it takes to get them to remove all of the items that you request will vary from person to person. One person may send letter #1 and get virtually all of the negative items removed in less than 30 days. Another person may send letter #2 and only get a few accounts removed. Or a 3rd person may send out letter #1 and get the credit bureaus standard denial form letter or their intimidation denial letter.

Regardless of the results you get, it is important to be diligent and persistent. If, after the first "round" of letter #1's there is still derogatory information remaining on your credit report then you simply send the next letter that I give you in this book and emphasizing that it is your "2nd" written request for them to send you copies of their verifiable proof the amount in question or have the item deleted as per section 609.

Eventually, you will find that all of your derogatory accounts will begin to disappear. For some people, it happens quickly and is quite easy and to others it can be a fight and take much longer.

IMPORTANT: The reason I found that the time it takes to get your disputed items removed varies from person to person is because most dispute letters never get read by a "real human." The trick is to get the letter read by a real human instead of a computer. Here's how it works:

Initially your dispute letter goes to a human, but he/she doesn't read it. They only open the envelope and then run the page or pages through a computerized scanner. The scanning machine does an optical recognition of the words in your letter. If your letter is type written, then the name of the creditor and the account numbers that you are disputing can be read by the computer and they are compared to the creditor name and the account numbers in your credit file and if they match up, then the computer automatically sends you a form letter stating that **"the account information has been verified".**

Most people give up after they receive a reply from the credit bureau stating that they have verified the account to be accurate. That is easy to do right? Considering that you know that the account belongs to you. Most people are expecting this credit dispute process not to work so they quit as soon as they receive this reply from the credit bureau. That's what the credit bureaus want you to do. Don't Quit!

So, the key is to make sure that your dispute letter gets rejected by the computer and passed on to a real live person. So, how do I do that?

I simply recommend that you hand-write in the creditors name and account numbers rather than type them in on your letter. (See sample letters in this book that illustrates what I mean). Now handwriting this portion of the letter does not guarantee that the human who is going to look (notice I said "look" not read) at your dispute letter is going to automatically delete the items that you are disputing because he or she sees that you are disputing their "right to report" not the accuracy of the item.

Without getting into a whole lot of details of the duties and restrictions put on employees at the credit bureaus and to make a long story short, it suffices to say that these people have to deal with thousands of files each day, which means that they can only spend a few minutes per file if they are going to make their quota each day. So even though you got your dispute letter past the computer and into the hands of a real live person these people may still ignore your letter and automatically get the computer to send you another type of "form letter" we call the "Intimidation Form Letter Rejection". Experian, Equifax or TransUnion may send you a communication saying something like this:

"We received a suspicious looking request regarding your personal credit information that we have determined was not sent by you. We have not taken any action on this request and any future requests made in this manner will not be processed and will not receive a response."

Or you may receive a letter back from them that asks you, if you are doing business with a credit repair company or whether or not you paid a company to help you draft up your dispute letter and they may ask you to fill out a questionnaire and return it to them before they will review your dispute. **DO NOT FILL OUT ANYTHING** and return it to them. **ONLY use the letters in this book**.

These types of intimidating responses are designed to discourage you and/or scare you into believing that you are doing something wrong and get you to abandon your dispute. Credit bureaus do not like it when consumers file disputes because it costs them time and money to do it even if they just mail you back a "rejection form letter". They get tens of thousands of letters a day which translates into hundreds of thousands of dollars to deal with them. The sooner they scare you away or discourage you away the better it is for their profits.

To further scare you into submission, they may also include something like this:

"Suspicious requests are taken seriously and reviewed by security personnel who will report deceptive activity, including copies of letters deemed as suspicious, to law enforcement officials and to state or federal regulatory agencies."

If you notice with each of the Section 609 Affidavit Credit Dispute Letters, you are including a notarized copy of your Driver's License and/or a picture ID card, and a copy of your Social Security Card.

Because Section 610(a)(1) [ε 1681 h] of the FCRA stipulates that a credit bureau is only required to respond to a dispute from a consumer, if it is in writing and if the consumer properly verifies that they are who they say they are using proper identification. A copy of a valid driver license showing an address that matches up with the address showing on your credit report and a copy of your social security card are considered valid identification. By providing all of this information, there is no question whatsoever that YOU are the one making the written request.

IMPORTANT: Make sure that the address showing on your driver license is the same address that shows up on your credit report. If it doesn't, then I highly recommend that you go down to the DMV and tell them that you lost your driver's license and order a new one with the proper address on it. If you don't tell them that you lost your old card, they will simply issue you a change of address card which the credit bureaus may not accept; therefore, it is wise to have your proper address showing on the card itself. Sometimes if the address on your driver's license doesn't match up, then, they will accept a copy of two utility bills that shows your name and address, which match up with the same name and address showing on your credit report.

Also note that if you do not have a copy of your SSN card, make a copy of a pay stub or W–2 form that shows your name and SSN on it.

Before starting the dispute process, you should go down to the FedEx Store, or your local copy center and get about 12-15 copies made with both your driver's license and SS card so that you have them available when it is time to start mailing dispute letters and responding to their delay or intimidation letters.

Remember, if you do happen to get some resistance from the Credit Bureaus – don't be alarmed and DO NOT give up. They don't play fair and very seldom do they comply after only receiving your first letter. If they send you a rejection or an intimidation letter, as I discussed earlier, just send the next letter and remind them it is your 2nd request!

If they send you a form to fill out and return to them DON'T fill out any forms and return it to them. Only use the letters that are in this book. Keep sending the letters DEMANDING the Credit Bureau either provide the verifiable proof or DELETE the item. It may take a few letters and determined persistence, but all "unverified" items must and will be deleted.

In the extreme case where the CRA's try to ignore your multiple written requests, you can file a lawsuit and sue the CRA for damages under the Fair Credit Reporting Act (FCRA) and/or file a formal complaint with the Federal Trade Commission (www.ftc.gov) for violations of the FCRA. You can file your complaint here:

https://www.ftccomplaintassistant.gov

One more thing, it is recommended that you Do Not Apply For any additional credit during the dispute process and do not allow anybody to pull your credit during this time either.... UNLESS it is absolutely necessary.

If you are presently in debt and are unable to make all of your monthly payments to any or all of your creditors, then you need to know how to deal with these creditors. This is critical not only to the credit dispute process, but it is critical that you not speak to any debt collector over the phone. You must only communicate with them in writing.

If you only communicate with them in writing and you do it properly, then there is an excellent chance that you will be able to walk away from that outstanding debt without getting sued and without having to pay any of the money back. If you are in this situation, then you need to deny all debt.

Under Federal Law, once per year, you can receive a FREE credit report from each of the three main Credit Reporting Agencies.

Step 1: Pull a Credit Report from Experian, Equifax & TransUnion

Go to: http://www.annualcreditreport.com to get copies of your FREE credit reports. If you are lucky, you will be able to access all three credit reports online immediately. But beware. Your online request might get denied because they say that they cannot verify that you are who say you are. If that is the case, don't give up. Simply print out the forms that comes up on your screen and fill it out and mail it to the address that is on the form and include a copy of your driver's license and SS card as proof of identification. It will only take a few days and you will either receive a copy of your credit report in the mail and/or, they will mail you a link to go to that will enable you to download a copy of you report.

(Note: if you have already used your free report for the year–you may have to purchase a new report).

Step 2: Review Each Credit Report & Identify All of The NEGATIVE Items That You Want to Be Removed. Make A List: (See sample below)

Name of Account: Account Number:

1.   Chase Bank 533376304023...
2.   B of A 424492101261...
3.   Palisades Collection PAL3CHSARB8275...
4.   Midland 3452676554422525

NOTE #1: The negative accounts that you want to have deleted are easy to find. Usually there will be a section on your credit report titled: **The Following Accounts that may be considered negative:**

NOTE #2: The account numbers listed for each account shown on your credit report are always partial account numbers. Don't worry. That is all you need to write onto your dispute letters. Simply write in the same partial account number beside the Name of Account as per the illustrations above.

After you complete your list, **you'll be "Hand-Writing" both the Name of Account and the Account Number onto the letter.** Remember, that is important if you want to get your dispute letter seen and read by a real live person, which increases the chances of getting the negative item removed with the first letter or 2nd letter.

After you have compiled your list of negatives for each credit report, you will need to open the Section 609 Affidavit Credit Dispute **Letter #1** for the first credit bureau. **Do this one credit-bureau-at-a-time.**

NOTE #3: Before you start, I recommend that you create 3 separate folders.

1. Experian
2. Equifax
3. Trans Union

Then copy each of the letters #1, #2, #3 and #4 for each of the folders. Then, let's start with Experian. Plug in your name, address, etc., then Print out the letter and **then hand write in the accounts and the partial account numbers** for each account that you want deleted and also add the word "Unverified Account". See example below:

Name of Account: Account Number: Provide Physical Proof of Verification

1.   Chase Bank #533376304023… Unverified Account

I have also provided a real sample of my own section 609 credit affidavit disputes.

Corey Pishon Smith
3792 Brookmeade Street
Memphis, Tennessee 38127
SSN: ~~████████~~
DOB: 11/20/1973

May 30, 2012

Equifax Information Services
P.O. Box 740256
Atlanta, GA 30374

This letter is my formal written request for you to investigate the following "Unverified" accounts listed below: According to the Fair Credit Reporting Act, 15 U.S.C. § 1681 your company is required by federal law to verify - through the physical verification of the original signed consumer contract - any and all accounts you post on a credit report to assure maximum accuracy. Without proper verification by your company, anyone paying for your reporting services could fax, mail or email in a fraudulent account.

I demand to see a copy of the Verifiable Proof (an original Consumer Contract with my Signature on it) that you used to verify that the account belonged to me the first time you reported the account on my credit report. Your failure to properly verify these accounts has hurt my ability to obtain credit. Under the FCRA 15 U.S.C. § 1681, unverified accounts must be promptly deleted. If you are unable to provide me with a copy of the verifiable proof that you have on file within 30 days for each of the accounts listed below then you must remove these accounts from my credit report. Please provide me with a copy of an updated and corrected credit report showing these items removed.

I demand the following accounts be verified or removed immediately.

Name of Account:	Account Number:		Provide Physical Proof of Verification
US Department of Education	#3200705002680	08/1999	Unverified Account
US Department of Education	#3200705002680	10/1996	Unverified Account
US Department of Education	#3200705002680	08/1997	Unverified Account
US Department of Education	#3200705002680	08/1997	Unverified Account
US Department of Education	#3200705002680	08/1998	Unverified Account
US Department of Education	#3200705002680	10/1996	Unverified Account
US Department of Education	#3200705002680	08/1997	Unverified Account
US Department of Education	#3200705002680	08/1999	Unverified Account
US Department of Education	#3200705002679	08/1998	Unverified Account
US Department of Edu AFsa	#410151*	08/1996	Unverified Account

* Please also remove all non-account holding inquiries over 30 days old.

Thank You,

Corey P. Smith

Corey P. Smith

50

[signature of affiant]

Corey Phshon Smith
3792 Brookmeade St.
Memphis, TN 38127

Subscribed and sworn to before me, this 30th day of May, 2012.

NOTARY SEAL:

[signature of Notary]

Niki Macklin
[print name of Notary]

NOTARY PUBLIC

My commission expires:
_____2-23_____, 20_12_.

<u>Attached</u>: Copy of my Social Security Card & Drivers License is attached
Sent: USPS Certified Mail

P. O. Box 105518
Atlanta, GA 30348

001227310-11857
011857
Corey Smith
#92 Promenade St
Memphis, TN 38127-4656

EQUIFAX

CREDIT FILE : August 31, 2012
Confirmation # 2223034845

Dear Corey Smith:

Below are the results of your reinvestigation request and, as applicable, any revisions to your credit file. If you have additional questions regarding the reinvestigated items, please contact the source of that information directly. You may also contact Equifax regarding the specific information contained within this letter or report within the next 60 days by visiting us at www.investigate.equifax.com or by calling a Customer Representative at (888) 855-4631 from 9:00am to 5:00pm Monday-Friday in your time zone.

Thank you for giving Equifax the opportunity to serve you.

The Results Of Our Reinvestigation

>>> We have reviewed your concerns and our conclusions are:

Paid as agreed accounts that have been paid in full will automatically be deleted ten years after date of last activity.
Adverse accounts that have been paid in full will automatically be deleted seven years from the date of last activity.

Credit Account Information
(For your security, the last 4 digits of account number(s) have been replaced by 'x')
This section includes open and closed accounts reported by credit grantors.

Account History		
1 : 30-59 Days Past Due	5 : 150-179 Days Past Due	J : Voluntary Surrender
2 : 60-89 Days Past Due	6 : 180 or More Days Past Due	K : Repossession
3 : 90-119 Days Past Due	G : Collection Account	L : Charge Off
4 : 120-149 Days Past Due,	H : Foreclosure	

Status Code
Descriptions

>>> We have researched the credit account. Account # - 3200705002680* The results are: This item has been deleted from the credit file. If you have additional questions about this item please contact: US Department of Education, PO Box 5609, Greenville TX 75403-5609 Phone: (800) 621-3115

>>> We have researched the credit account. Account # - 3200705002680* The results are: We verified that this item belongs to you. Additional information has been provided from the original source regarding this item. If you have additional questions about this item please contact: US Department of Education, PO Box 5609, Greenville TX 75403-5609 Phone: (800) 621-3115

>>> We have researched the credit account. Account # - 3200705002680* The results are: This item has been deleted from the credit file. If you have additional questions about this item please contact: US Department of Education, PO Box 5609, Greenville TX 75403-5609 Phone: (800) 621-3115

>>> We have researched the credit account. Account # - 410151* The results are: We verified that this item belongs to you. Additional information has been provided from the original source regarding this item. If you have additional questions about this item please contact: Direct Loans, PO Box 7202, Utica NY 13504-7202

(Continued On Next Page)

Page 1 of 4

2223034845IB4-001227310- 11857- 12018 - AS

52

CREDIT FILE : August 31, 2012

Confirmation # 222303484S

US Department of Edu Also: PO BOX 7202, UTICA NY 13504-7202

Account Number		Date Opened	High Credit	Credit Limit	Terms Duration	Terms Frequency		Months Revd	Activity Designator		Creditor Classification	
410151*		08/31/1996	$60,949	$0	120 Months			5				
Items As of	Balance	Date of	Actual	Scheduled	Date of 1st	Date of	Date Maj.	Charge Off	Deferred Pay	Balloon Pay		Date
Date Reported	Amount	Last Pymnt	Payment Amount	Payment Amount	Delinquency	Last Activity	Del. 1st Paid	Amount	Start Date	Amount		Closed
08/31/2012	$0	11/2006	$0	$0	01/2006	01/2006		$0		$0		11/2006

Status - Collection Account; Type of Account - Installment; Type of Loan - Education Loan; Whose Account - Individual Account; ADDITIONAL INFORMATION - Collection Account; Claim Filed With Government;

Account History with Status Codes

12/2005	11/2006	10/2006	09/2006	08/2006	07/2006	06/2006	05/2006	04/2006	03/2006	02/2006	01/2006
4	4	4	4	4	4	4	4	4	3	2	

>>> *We have researched the credit account. Account # - 3200705002680* The results are:* This item has been deleted from the credit file. If you have additional questions about this item please contact: *US Department of Education, PO Box 5609, Greenville TX 75403-5609 Phone: (800) 621-3115*

>>> *We have researched the credit account. Account # - 3200705002679* The results are:* This item has been deleted from the credit file. If you have additional questions about this item please contact: *US Department of Education, PO Box 5609, Greenville TX 75403-5609 Phone: (800) 621-3115*

>>> *We have researched the credit account. Account # - 410151* The results are:* We verified that this item belongs to you. If you have additional questions about this item please contact: *Direct Loans, PO Box 7202, Utica NY 13504-7202*

US Department of Edu Also: PO BOX 7202, UTICA NY 13504-7202

Account Number		Date Opened	High Credit	Credit Limit	Terms Duration	Terms Frequency		Months Revd	Activity Designator		Creditor Classification	
410151*		12/31/2010	$96,057	$0	360 Months	Deferred		6		Paid and Closed		
Items As of	Balance	Date of	Actual	Scheduled	Date of 1st	Date of	Date Maj.	Charge Off	Deferred Pay	Balloon Pay		Date
Date Reported	Amount	Last Payment	Paymnt Amount	Payment Amount	Delinquency	Last Activity	Del. 1st Pymd	Amount	Start Date	Amount		Closed
08/31/2012	$0		$0	$396		02/2011		$0		$0		09/2011

Status - Pays As Agreed; Type of Account - Installment; Type of Loan - Education Loan; Whose Account - Individual Account; ADDITIONAL INFORMATION - Closed or Paid Account/Zero Balance; Student Loan;

>>> *We have researched the credit account. Account # - 3200705002680* The results are:* This item has been deleted from the credit file. If you have additional questions about this item please contact: *US Department of Education, PO Box 5609, Greenville TX 75403-5609 Phone: (800) 621-3115*

>>> *We have researched the credit account. Account # - 3200705002680* The results are:* This item has been deleted from the credit file. If you have additional questions about this item please contact: *US Department of Education, PO Box 5609, Greenville TX 75403-5609 Phone: (800) 621-3115*

>>> *We have researched the credit account. Account # - 3200705002680* The results are:* This item has been deleted from the credit file. If you have additional questions about this item please contact: *US Department of Education, PO Box 5609, Greenville TX 75403-5609 Phone: (800) 621-3115*

>>> *We have researched the credit account. Account # - 3200705002680* The results are:* This item has been deleted from the credit file. If you have additional questions about this item please contact: *US Department of Education, PO Box 5609, Greenville TX 75403-5609 Phone: (800) 621-3115*

222303484S|B4-001227310-11857-1201P

53

NOTE #4: I've used a handwriting font in the example above——You should actually handwrite this onto the letter and slant the line a bit so it is not straight in case you have neat handwriting. Otherwise, the scanner will probably be able to read the handwriting font whereas it is unlikely it will be able to read your own handwriting, especially if you use a blue ink pen and the lines are slanted a bit or crooked.

NOTE #5: If you have more than 22 negative accounts on your credit report, make sure that you **Only dispute a maximum of 22 accounts at one time**. Attempting to dispute more than 22 accounts at one time could cause the Credit Bureaus to classify your dispute as frivolous and do nothing. They have the right to do that.

STEP 3: Attach a copy of your Social Security Card & Driver's License to each letter that you send them including letter #2 etc.

Once you complete each letter, simply get the letter notarized, include a photocopy of our Social Security Card and ID card (Driver's License or Passport) as proof of your identity and mail the letter to the credit bureau **CERTIFIED MAIL**. (This will enable you to track delivery of your letter and provide proof that it was received by the Credit Bureau) if they end up doing nothing. That would be nice considering they would have to delete all of the items you requested once you showed them or the court your proof of delivery.

STEP 4: Hand write the envelope, don't type.

Handwrite your return address and the Credit Bureau address on the envelope so the credit bureau treats the dispute letter as if it is from an individual which means that they are more than likely to take longer to open your letter, which means they will take longer to deal with it and with that being said, there is a better chance that they'll remove the items quicker.

The 3rd world workers who deal with dispute letters have strict quota rules to abide by if they want to keep their job. So, when they get behind they have two options: 1) Send out the "we have verified form letter" to the stack of letters that they are behind on. 2) Or, delete all of the disputed items on the stack of letters that they are behind on. Envelopes that are hand–written are taken as letters from individual consumers and are dealt with last, which means that when they get around to opening them, a week may have already gone by. Since they have to respond to your dispute within 30 days, they quite often don't have time to deal with your dispute, so you have a 50/50 chance of getting the items removed with the first letter.

Step 5: Wait 2 Days then prepare and mail out Letter #1 to the 2nd Credit Bureau and then 4 days later mail letter #1 to the 3rd credit bureau.

Don't send out your dispute letter #1 to all 3 credit bureaus on the same day. Send them out *four days apart*. Doing it this way increases the odds of getting the items removed after only using the first letter.

After you mail out letter #1 to all 3 credit bureaus over a nine-day period then you'll watch your mail closely for responses from the credit bureaus. It usually takes about 21-30 days to receive your first correspondence from the credit bureaus. As I have written previously, they will send you anything from a copy of your credit report to an "intimidation letter". If you receive a response and some negative items were not removed AND the Credit Bureau DID NOT provide you with a copy of the written verifiable proof per your written request – then send the next letter. It is recommended that you keep (3) file folders – one for Equifax, Experian and TransUnion and keep very detailed records of the dates of your communications with each Credit Reporting Agency. It is important that you establish a paper trail history of your efforts to enforce your consumer rights under the Fair Credit Reporting Act. **DOCUMENT EVERYTHING IN WRITING.** Keep copies of letters, certified mail receipts, response letters, and notes. I have provided an example of how each affidavit should be written.

Your Full Name (Make sure it matches the name on your credit report)

Address

City, State Zip

SSN: 000-00-0000 | DOB: 7/1/1960

Equifax

P.O. Box 740256

Atlanta, GA 30374

    This letter is my formal written request for you to investigate the following "Unverified" accounts listed below: According to the Fair Credit Reporting Act, **15 U.S.C. § 1681 your company is required by federal law to verify** - through the physical verification of the original signed consumer contract - any and all accounts you post on a credit report to assure maximum accuracy. Without proper verification by your company, anyone paying for your reporting services could fax, mail or email in a fraudulent account.

    I demand to see a copy of the Verifiable Proof (**an original Consumer Contract with my Signature on it**) that you used to verify that the account belonged to me the first time you reported the account on my credit report. Your failure to properly verify these accounts has hurt my ability to obtain credit.   Under the **FCRA 15 U.S.C. § 1681**, unverified accounts <u>must be promptly deleted</u>. If you are unable to provide me with a copy of the verifiable proof that you have on file within 30 days for each of the accounts listed below then you must remove these accounts from my credit report. Please provide me with a copy of an updated and corrected credit report showing these items removed.

I demand the following accounts be verified or removed immediately.

<u>Name of Account:</u>	<u>Account Number:</u>	<u>Provide Physical Proof of Verification</u>
1. Chase Bank	#533376304023 …	Unverified Account

(Hand Write this information with blue ink pen)

Make sure that you don't have more than 22 accounts listed

* Please also remove all **non-account holding inquiries** over 30 days old.

Thank You,

Sign your name here

(Your Name Here)

Attached: Copy of my Social Security Card & Driver's License is attached

Sent: USPS Certified Mail

Take these cards down to your copy center and make clear copies of both on one sheet. They must be legible or else the credit bureaus will reject them.

COPY of SSN CARD

COPY OF ID CARD

February 1, 2012

Your Name

Address

City, State Zip

SSN: 000-00-0000 | DOB: 1/1/1960

Equifax

P.O. Box 740256

Atlanta, GA 30374

Please be advised that this is my <u>SECOND WRITTEN REQUEST</u> for you to remove the unverified accounts listed below that remain on my credit report in violation of 15 U.S.C. § 1681. You are required under the FCRA to have properly verified that an account listed on my credit report is mine by having a copy of the original credit application on file. In the results of your first re-investigation, you stated in writing that you **"verified"** that these items are being **"reported correctly". Who in your company verified these account: How did they verify them? Please provide me with the name of the individual, business address, and telephone number of the person or business contacted during your re-investigation.** Also, tell me why didn't you send me copies of the verification like I asked you to?

As I am sure that you are well aware, current case law states that, Consumer Reporting Agencies bear grave responsibilities to ensure the accuracy of the accounts they report on and their responsibility must consi of something more than merely parroting information received from other sources. The Courts have ordered that a "Reinvestigation" that merely shifts the burden back to the consumer and the credit grantor cannot fulfill the obligations imposed by § 1681(a)(4).

You have **NOT** provided me a copy of ANY original documentation that you have on file that is required under **Section 609 & Section 611 (a)(1)(A)** (a consumer contract with my signature on it) and under **Section 611 (5)(A)** of the FCRA – you are required to **"...promptly DELETE all information which cannot be verified."**

The law is very clear as to the Civil liability and the remedy available to me for "negligent noncomplianc (**Section 617**) if you fail to comply with this Federal Law. **I am a litigious consumer and fully intend on pursuing litigation in this matter to enforce my rights under the FCRA. I demand the following accoun be verified or deleted immediately.**

Name of Account:	Account Number:	Provide Physical Proof of Verification
1. Chase Bank	#533376304023 ...	Unverified Account

59

(Hand Write this information with blue ink pen)

Note: If they have already removed some of the items that you listed on your first letter than remove them from your list on this letter.

Thanking you in advance for your anticipated quick co-operation on this matter.

Thank you,

Your Signature Here

Your Name Here

[signature of affiant]

John Doe
2222 Brook Meade St.
Memphis, TN 38127

Subscribed and sworn to before me, this 30th day of April, 2012.

NOTARY SEAL:

[signature of Notary]

[print name of Notary]

NOTARY PUBLIC

My commission expires:
_____, 20_____.

Attached: Copy of my Social Security Card & Driver's License is attached

Sent: USPS Certified Mail

COPY of SSN CARD

COPY OF ID CARD

February 1, 2012

Your Name

Address

City, State Zip

SSN: 000-00-0000 | DOB: 1/1/1970

Equifax

P.O. Box 740256

Atlanta, GA 30374

Please be advised that this is my <u>THIRD WRITTEN REQUEST</u> and FINAL WARNING that I fully intend to pursue litigation in accordance with the FCRA to enforce my rights and seek relief and recove all monetary damages that I may be entitled to under Section 616 and Section 617 regarding your continued willful and negligent noncompliance.

Despite two written requests, the unverified items listed below still remain on my credit report in violation Federal Law. You are required under the FCRA to have properly verified that an account listed on my credit file is mine by having a copy of the original credit application on file. In the results of your first investigation and subsequent reinvestigation, you stated in writing that you **"verified"** that these items are being **"reported correctly".** Who in your company verified these accounts are mine? How did they verify them? You still have not provided me with the name of the individual, business address, and telephone number of the person or business contacted during your re-investigation. You have **NOT** provided me with a copy of ANY original documentation (a credit application with my signature on it) **as** required under **Section 609 & Section 611 (a)(1)(A).** Furthermore, you have failed to provide the method of verification as required under **Section 611 (a) (7).** Please be advised that under **Section 611 (5)(A)** of the FCRA – you are required to *"...promptly DELET all information which cannot be verified."*

The law is very clear as to the Civil liability and the remedy available to me (**Section 616 & 617**) if you fa to comply with Federal Law. I am a litigious consumer and fully intend on pursuing litigation in this matter to enforce my rights under the FCRA.

I demand that you send me copies of the documents you used to verify the following accounts list below or you delete them immediately. Please provide me with a copy of an updated and correct credit report showing that these items have been deleted.

Name of Account:	Account Number:	Provide Physical Proof of Verification
1. Chase Bank	#533376304023 ...	Unverified Account

(Hand Write this information with blue ink pen)

Note: If they have already removed some of the items that you listed on your first & second letter than remove them from your list on this letter.

Thanking you in advance for your anticipated quick co-operation on this matter.

Thank you,

Your Signature Here

Your Name Here

_____

[signature of affiant]

John Doe
2222 Brook Meade St.
Memphis, TN 38127

Subscribed and sworn to before me, this 30th day of April, 2012.

NOTARY SEAL:

_____

[signature of Notary]

_____

[print name of Notary]

NOTARY PUBLIC

My commission expires:
_____, 20_____.

Attached: Copy of my Social Security Card & Driver's License is attached

Sent: USPS Certified Mail

COPY of SSN CARD

COPY OF ID CARD

Your Name

Address

City, State Zip

SSN: 000-00-0000 | DOB: 1/1/1960

Equifax

P.O. Box 740256

Atlanta, GA 30374

NOTICE OF PENDING LITIGATION SEEKING RELIEF AND MONETARY DAMAGES UNDER FCRA SECTION 616 & SECTION 617

Please accept this final written **OFFER OF SETTLEMENT BEFORE LITIGATION** as my attempt to amicably resolve your continued violation of the Fair Credit Reporting Act regarding your refusal to delete all of the UNVERIFIED account information from my consumer file.

Your failure to provide me with verifiable proof required to post the accounts listed below proves that it does not exist and is therefore "Unverified". I intend to pursue litigation in accordance with the FCRA to seek relief and recover all monetary damages that I may be entitled to under Section 616 and Section 617 if the UNVERIFIED items listed below are not deleted within 10 days.   A copy of this letter as well as copies of the three written letters sent to you previously will also become part of a formal complaint to the Federal Trade Commission and also shall be used as evidence in pending litigation provided you fail to comply with this offer of settlement.

Despite my three written requests, the unverified items listed below still remain on my credit report in violation of Federal Law. In the results of your investigations, you stated in writing that you **"verified"** that these items are being **"reported correctly"?** Who verified these accounts? How did they verify them? You still have not provided me with the name of the individual, business address, and telephone number of the person or business contacted during your re-investigation. You have **NOT** provided me a copy of ANY original documentation (a consumer contract with my signature on it. Furthermore, you have failed to provide the method of verification as required under **Section 611 (a) (7)**.   Please be advised that under **Section 611 (5)(A)** of the FCRA – you are required to *"…promptly DELETE all information which cannot be verified."*

The law is very clear as to the Civil liability and the remedy available to me (**Section 616 & 617**) if you fail to comply with Federal Law. I am a litigious consumer and fully intend on pursuing litigation in this matter to enforce my rights under the FCRA.

In order to avoid legal action, I demand that you send me copies of the documents you used to verify the following accounts listed below or you delete them immediately. Please provide me with a copy of an updated and corrected credit report showing that these items have been deleted.

Name of Account:	Account Number:	Provide Physical Proof of Verification
1. Chase Bank	#533376304023 ...	Unverified Account

(Hand Write this information with blue ink pen)

Note: If they have already removed some of the items that you listed on your first & second letter than remove them from your list on this letter.

Thank you,

Your Signature Here

Your Name Here

_____
[signature of affiant]

John Doe
2222 Brook Meade St.
Memphis, TN 38127

Subscribed and sworn to before me, this 30th day of April, 2012.

NOTARY SEAL:

_____
[signature of Notary]

_____
[print name of Notary]

NOTARY PUBLIC

My commission expires:
_____, 20_____.

Attached: Copy of my Social Security Card & Driver's License is attached

<u>Sent</u>: USPS Certified Mail

COPY of SSN CARD

COPY OF ID CARD

February 1, 2012

Your Name

Address

City, State Zip

SSN: 000-00-0000 | DOB: 1/1/1960

Equifax

P.O. Box 740256

Atlanta, GA 30374

NOTICE OF PENDING LITIGATION SEEKING RELIEF AND MONETARY DAMAGES UNDER FCRA SECTION 616 & SECTION 617

Please accept this final written OFFER OF SETTLEMENT BEFORE LITIGATION as my attempt to amicably resolve your continued violation of the Fair Credit Reporting Act regarding your refusal to delete all of the UNVERIFIED account information from my consumer file.

Your failure to provide me with verifiable proof required to post the accounts listed below proves that it does not exist and is therefore "Unverified". I intend to pursue litigation in accordance with the FCRA to seek relief and recover all monetary damages that I may be entitled to under Section 616 and Section 617 if the UNVERIFIED items listed below are not deleted within 10 days.   A copy of this letter as well as copies of the three written letters sent to you previously will also become part of a formal complaint to the Federal Trade Commission and also shall be used as evidence in pending litigation provided you fail to comply with this offer of settlement.

Despite my three written requests, the unverified items listed below still remain on my credit report in violation of Federal Law. In the results of your investigations, you stated in writing that you **"verified"** that these items are being **"reported correctly"**?   Who verified these accounts?   How did they verify them? You still have not provided me with the name of the individual, business address, and telephone number of the person or business contacted during your re-investigation. You have **NOT** provided me a copy of ANY original documentation (a consumer contract with my signature on it. Furthermore, you have failed to provide the method of verification as required under **Section 611 (a) (7)**.   Please be advised that under **Section 611 (5)(A)** of the FCRA – you are required to *"...promptly DELETE all information which cannot be verified."*

The law is very clear as to the Civil liability and the remedy available to me (**Section 616 & 617**) if you fail to comply with Federal Law. I am a litigious consumer and fully intend on pursuing litigation in this matter to enforce my rights under the FCRA.

In order to avoid legal action, I demand that you send me copies of the documents you used to verify the following accounts listed below or you delete them immediately. Please provide me with a copy of an updated and corrected credit report showing that these items have been deleted.

Name of Account:	Account Number:	Provide Physical Proof of Verification
1. Chase Bank	#533376304023 ...	Unverified Account

(Hand Write this information with blue ink pen)

Note: If they have already removed some of the items that you listed on your first & second letter than remove them from your list on this letter.

Thank you,

Your Signature Here

Your Name Here

_____
[signature of affiant]

John Doe
2222 Brook Meade St.
Memphis, TN 38127

Subscribed and sworn to before me, this 30th day of April, 2012.

NOTARY SEAL:

_____
[signature of Notary]

_____
[print name of Notary]

NOTARY PUBLIC

My commission expires:
_____, 20_____.

Attached: Copy of my Social Security Card & Driver's License is attached

<u>Sent</u>: USPS Certified Mail

COPY of SSN CARD

COPY OF ID CARD

February 1, 2012

Your Name

Address

City, State Zip

SSN: 000-00-0000 | DOB: 1/1/1960

Experian

P.O. Box 2002

Allen, TX 75013

Please be advised that this is my <u>SECOND WRITTEN REQUEST</u> for you to remove the unverified accounts listed below that remain on my credit report in violation of 15 U.S.C. § 1681. You are required under the FCRA to have properly verified that an account listed on my credit report is mine by having a copy of the original credit application on file. In the results of your first re-investigation, you stated in writing that you **"verified"** that these items are being **"reported correctly". Who in your company verified these accounts? How did they verify them? Please provide me with the name of the individual, business address, and telephone number of the person or business contacted during your re-investigation.** Also, tell me why didn't you send me copies of the verification like I asked you to?

As I am sure that you are well aware, current case law states that, Consumer Reporting Agencies bear grave responsibilities to ensure the accuracy of the accounts they report on and their responsibility must consist of something more than merely parroting information received from other sources. The Courts have ordered that a "Reinvestigation" that merely shifts the burden back to the consumer and the credit grantor cannot fulfill the obligations imposed by § 1681(a)(4).

You have **NOT** provided me a copy of ANY original documentation that you have on file that is required under **Section 609 & Section 611 (a)(1)(A)** (a consumer contract with my signature on it) and under **Section 611 (5)(A)** of the FCRA – you are required to **"...promptly DELETE all information which cannot be verified."**

The law is very clear as to the Civil liability and the remedy available to me for "negligent noncompliance" (**Section 617**) if you fail to comply with this Federal Law. **I am a litigious consumer and fully intend on pursuing litigation in this matter to enforce my rights under the FCRA. I demand the following accounts be verified or deleted immediately.**

<u>Name of Account:</u>	<u>Account Number:</u>	<u>Provide Physical Proof of Verification</u>
1. Chase Bank	#533376304023 ...	Unverified Account

71

(Hand Write this information with blue ink pen)

Note: If they have already removed some of the items that you listed on your first letter than remove them from your list on this letter.

      Thanking you in advance for your anticipated quick co-operation on this matter.

Thank you,

Your Signature Here

Your Name Here

_____

[signature of affiant]

John Doe
2222 Brook Meade St.
Memphis, TN 38127

Subscribed and sworn to before me, this 30th day of April, 2012.

NOTARY SEAL:

_____

[signature of Notary]

_____

[print name of Notary]

NOTARY PUBLIC

My commission expires:
_____, 20_____.

Attached: Copy of my Social Security Card & Driver's License is attached

Sent: USPS Certified Mail

COPY of SSN CARD

COPY OF ID CARD

February 1, 2012

Your Name

Address

City, State Zip

SSN: 000-00-0000 | DOB: 1/1/1970

Experian

P.O. Box 2002

Allen, TX 75013

Please be advised that this is my THIRD WRITTEN REQUEST and FINAL WARNING that I fully intend to pursue litigation in accordance with the FCRA to enforce my rights and seek relief and recover all monetary damages that I may be entitled to under Section 616 and Section 617 regarding your continued willful and negligent noncompliance.

Despite two written requests, the unverified items listed below still remain on my credit report in violation of Federal Law. You are required under the FCRA to have properly verified that an account listed on my credit file is mine by having a copy of the original credit application on file. In the results of your first investigation and subsequent reinvestigation, you stated in writing that you "**verified**" that these items are being "**reported correctly**". Who in your company verified these accounts are mine? How did they verify them? You still have not provided me with the name of the individual, business address, and telephone number of the person or business contacted during your re-investigation. You have **NOT** provided me with a copy of ANY original documentation (a credit application with my signature on it) **as required under Section 609 & Section 611 (a)(1)(A).** Furthermore, you have failed to provide the method of verification as required under **Section 611 (a) (7)**. Please be advised that under **Section 611 (5)(A)** of the FCRA – you are required to *"...promptly DELETE all information which cannot be verified."*

The law is very clear as to the Civil liability and the remedy available to me (**Section 616 & 617**) if you fail to comply with Federal Law. I am a litigious consumer and fully intend on pursuing litigation in this matter to enforce my rights under the FCRA.

I demand that you send me copies of the documents you used to verify the following accounts listed below or you delete them immediately. Please provide me with a copy of an updated and corrected credit report showing that these items have been deleted.

Name of Account:	Account Number:	Provide Physical Proof of Verification
1. Chase Bank	#533376304023 ...	Unverified Account

(Hand Write this information with blue ink pen)

Note: If they have already removed some of the items that you listed on your first & second letter than remove them from your list on this letter.

Thanking you in advance for your anticipated quick co-operation on this matter.

Thank you,

Your Signature Here

Your Name Here

_____
[signature of affiant]

John Doe
22222 Brook Meade St.
Memphis, TN 38127

Subscribed and sworn to before me, this 30th day of April, 2012.

NOTARY SEAL:

_____
[signature of Notary]

_____
[print name of Notary]

NOTARY PUBLIC

My commission expires:
_____, 20_____.

<u>Attached</u>: Copy of my Social Security Card & Driver's License is attached

<u>Sent</u>: USPS Certified Mail

```
┌─────────────────────────────────────┐
│                                     │
│                                     │
│          COPY of SSN CARD           │
│                                     │
│                                     │
└─────────────────────────────────────┘
```

```
┌─────────────────────────────────────┐
│                                     │
│                                     │
│          COPY OF ID CARD            │
│                                     │
│                                     │
└─────────────────────────────────────┘
```

February 1, 2012

Your Name

Address

City, State Zip

SSN: 000-00-0000 | DOB: 1/1/1960

Experian

P.O. Box 2002

Allen, TX 75013

**NOTICE OF PENDING LITIGATION SEEKING RELIEF AND MONETARY DAMAGES UNDER FCRA
SECTION 616 & SECTION 617**

Please accept this final written **OFFER OF SETTLEMENT BEFORE LITIGATION** as my attempt to amicably resolve your continued violation of the Fair Credit Reporting Act regarding your refusal to delete all of the UNVERIFIED account information from my consumer file.

Your failure to provide me with verifiable proof required to post the accounts listed below proves that it does not exist and is therefore "Unverified". I intend to pursue litigation in accordance with the FCRA to seek relief and recover all monetary damages that I may be entitled to under Section 616 and Section 617 if the UNVERIFIED items listed below are not deleted within 10 days.   A copy of this letter as well as copies of the three written letters sent to you previously will also become part of a formal complaint to the Federal Trade Commission and also shall be used as evidence in pending litigation provided you fail to comply with this offer of settlement.

Despite my three written requests, the unverified items listed below still remain on my credit report in violation of Federal Law. In the results of your investigations, you stated in writing that you **"verified"** that these items are being **"reported correctly"?**   Who verified these accounts? How did they verify them? You still have not provided me with the name of the individual, business address, and telephone number of the person or business contacted during your re-investigation. You have **NOT** provided me a copy of ANY original documentation (a consumer contract with my signature on it. Furthermore, you have failed to provide the method of verification as required under **Section 611 (a) (7)**.   Please be advised that under **Section 611 (5)(A)** of the FCRA – you are required to *"...promptly DELETE all information which cannot be verified."*

The law is very clear as to the Civil liability and the remedy available to me (**Section 616 & 617**) if you fail to comply with Federal Law. I am a litigious consumer and fully intend on pursuing litigation in this matter to enforce my rights under the FCRA.

77

In order to avoid legal action, I demand that you send me copies of the documents you used to verify the following accounts listed below or you delete them immediately. Please provide me with a copy of an updated and corrected credit report showing that these items have been deleted.

Name of Account:	Account Number:	Provide Physical Proof of Verification
1. Chase Bank	#533376304023 …	Unverified Account

(Hand Write this information with blue ink pen)

Note: If they have already removed some of the items that you listed on your first & second letter than remove them from your list on this letter.

Thank you,

Your Signature Here

Your Name Here

_____
[signature of affiant]

John Doe
2222 Brook Meade St.
Memphis, TN 38127

Subscribed and sworn to before me, this 30th day of April, 2012.

NOTARY SEAL:

_____
[signature of Notary]

_____
[print name of Notary]

NOTARY PUBLIC

My commission expires:
_____, 20_____.

Attached: Copy of my Social Security Card & Driver's License is attached

<u>Sent</u>: USPS Certified Mail

COPY of SSN CARD

COPY OF ID CARD

February 1, 2012

Your Full Name (Make sure it matches the name on your credit report)

Address

City, State Zip

SSN: 000-00-0000 | DOB: 7/1/1960

Trans Union

P.O. Box 2000

Chester, PA 19022

　　　This letter is my formal written request for you to investigate the following "Unverified" accounts listed below: According to the Fair Credit Reporting Act, **15 U.S.C. § 1681 your company is required by federal law to verify** - through the physical verification of the original signed consumer contract - any and all accounts you post on a credit report to assure maximum accuracy. Without proper verification by your company, anyone paying for your reporting services could fax, mail or email in a fraudulent account.

　　　I demand to see a copy of the Verifiable Proof (**an original Consumer Contract with my Signature on it**) that you used to verify that the account belonged to me the first time you reported the account on my credit report. Your failure to properly verify these accounts has hurt my ability to obtain credit. Under the **FCRA 15 U.S.C. § 1681**, unverified accounts <u>must be promptly deleted</u>. If you are unable to provide me with a copy of the verifiable proof that you have on file within 30 days for each of the accounts listed below then you must remove these accounts from my credit report. Please provide me with a copy of an updated and corrected credit report showing these items removed.

I demand the following accounts be verified or removed immediately.

<u>Name of Account:</u>	<u>Account Number:</u>	<u>Provide Physical Proof of Verification</u>
1. Chase Bank	#533376304023 …	Unverified Account

(Hand Write this information with blue ink pen)

Make sure that you don't have more than 22 accounts listed

* Please also remove all **non-account holding inquiries** over 30 days old.

Thank You,

Sign your name here

(Your Name Here)

_____

[signature of affiant]

John Doe
2222 Brook Meade St.
Memphis, TN 38127

Subscribed and sworn to before me, this 30th day of April, 2012.

NOTARY SEAL:

_____

[signature of Notary]

_____

[print name of Notary]

NOTARY PUBLIC

My commission expires:
_____, 20_____.

Attached: Copy of my Social Security Card & Driver's License is attached

Sent: USPS Certified Mail

Take these cards down to your copy center and make clear copies of both on one sheet.

They must be legible or else the credit bureaus will reject them.

COPY of SSN CARD

COPY OF ID CARD

February 1, 2012

Your Name

Address

City, State Zip

SSN: 000-00-0000 | DOB: 1/1/1960

Trans Union

P.O. Box 2000

Chester, PA 19022

      Please be advised that this is my <u>SECOND WRITTEN REQUEST</u> for you to remove the unverified accounts listed below that remain on my credit report in violation of 15 U.S.C. § 1681. You are required under the FCRA to have properly verified that an account listed on my credit report is mine by having a copy of the original credit application on file. In the results of your first re-investigation, you stated in writing that you **"verified"** that these items are being **"reported correctly"**. **Who in your company verified these accounts? How did they verify them? Please provide me with the name of the individual, business address, and telephone number of the person or business contacted during your re-investigation.** Also, tell me why didn't you send me copies of the verification like I asked you to?

      As I am sure that you are well aware, current case law states that, Consumer Reporting Agencies bear grave responsibilities to ensure the accuracy of the accounts they report on and their responsibility must consist of something more than merely parroting information received from other sources. The Courts have ordered that a "Reinvestigation" that merely shifts the burden back to the consumer and the credit grantor cannot fulfill the obligations imposed by § 1681(a)(4).

      You have **NOT** provided me a copy of ANY original documentation that you have on file that is required under **Section 609 & Section 611 (a)(1)(A)** (a consumer contract with my signature on it) and under **Section 611 (5)(A)** of the FCRA – you are required to *"...promptly DELETE all information which cannot be verified."*

      The law is very clear as to the Civil liability and the remedy available to me for "negligent noncompliance" (**Section 617**) if you fail to comply with this Federal Law. **I am a litigious consumer and fully intend on pursuing litigation in this matter to enforce my rights under the FCRA. I demand the following accounts be verified or deleted immediately.**

Name of Account:	Account Number:	Provide Physical Proof of Verification
1. Chase Bank	#533376304023 ...	Unverified Account

(Hand Write this information with blue ink pen)

Note: If they have already removed some of the items that you listed on your first letter than remove them from your list on this letter.

Thanking you in advance for your anticipated quick co-operation on this matter.

Thank you,

Your Signature Here

Your Name Here

_____

[signature of affiant]

John Doe
2222 Brook Meade St.
Memphis, TN 38127

Subscribed and sworn to before me, this 30th day of April, 2012.

NOTARY SEAL:

_____

[signature of Notary]

_____

[print name of Notary]

NOTARY PUBLIC

My commission expires:
_____, 20_____.

Attached: Copy of my Social Security Card & Driver's License is attached

Sent: USPS Certified Mail

COPY of SSN CARD

COPY OF ID CARD

February 1, 2012

Your Name

Address

City, State Zip

SSN: 000-00-0000 | DOB: 1/1/1970

Trans Union

P.O. Box 2000

Chester, PA 19022

Please be advised that this is my THIRD WRITTEN REQUEST and FINAL WARNING that I fully intend to pursue litigation in accordance with the FCRA to enforce my rights and seek relief and recover all monetary damages that I may be entitled to under Section 616 and Section 617 regarding your continued willful and negligent noncompliance.

Despite two written requests, the unverified items listed below still remain on my credit report in violation of Federal Law. You are required under the FCRA to have properly verified that an account listed on my credit file is mine by having a copy of the original credit application on file. In the results of your first investigation and subsequent reinvestigation, you stated in writing that you **"verified"** that these items are being **"reported correctly"**. Who in your company verified these accounts are mine? How did they verify them? You still have not provided me with the name of the individual, business address, and telephone number of the person or business contacted during your re-investigation. You have **NOT** provided me with a copy of ANY original documentation (a credit application with my signature on it) **as** required under **Section 609 & Section 611 (a)(1)(A)**. Furthermore, you have failed to provide the method of verification as required under **Section 611 (a) (7)**. Please be advised that under **Section 611 (5)(A)** of the FCRA – you are required to **"...promptly DELETE all information which cannot be verified."**

The law is very clear as to the Civil liability and the remedy available to me (**Section 616 & 617**) if you fail to comply with Federal Law. I am a litigious consumer and fully intend on pursuing litigation in this matter to enforce my rights under the FCRA.

I demand that you send me copies of the documents you used to verify the following accounts listed below or you delete them immediately. Please provide me with a copy of an updated and corrected credit report showing that these items have been deleted.

Name of Account:	Account Number:	Provide Physical Proof of Verification
1. Chase Bank	#533376304023 ...	Unverified Account

(Hand Write this information with blue ink pen)

Note: If they have already removed some of the items that you listed on your first & second letter than remove them from your list on this letter.

Thanking you in advance for your anticipated quick co-operation on this matter.

Thank you,

Your Signature Here

Your Name Here

_____

[signature of affiant]

John Doe
2222 Brook Meade St.
Memphis, TN 38127

Subscribed and sworn to before me, this 30th day of April, 2012.

NOTARY SEAL:

_____

[signature of Notary]

_____

[print name of Notary]

NOTARY PUBLIC

My commission expires:
_____, 20_____.

Attached: Copy of my Social Security Card & Driver's License is attached

Sent: USPS Certified Mail

COPY of SSN CARD

COPY OF ID CARD

February 1, 2012

Your Name

Address

City, State Zip

SSN: 000-00-0000 | DOB: 1/1/1960

Trans Union

P.O. Box # 2000

Chester, PA. 19022

NOTICE OF PENDING LITIGATION SEEKING RELIEF AND MONETARY DAMAGES UNDER FCRA SECTION 616 & SECTION 617

Please accept this final written **OFFER OF SETTLEMENT BEFORE LITIGATION** as my attempt to amicably resolve your continued violation of the Fair Credit Reporting Act regarding your refusal to delete all of the UNVERIFIED account information from my consumer file.

Your failure to provide me with verifiable proof required to post the accounts listed below proves that it does not exist and is therefore "Unverified". I intend to pursue litigation in accordance with the FCRA to seek relief and recover all monetary damages that I may be entitled to under Section 616 and Section 617 if the UNVERIFIED items listed below are not deleted within 10 days.   A copy of this letter as well as copies of the three written letters sent to you previously will also become part of a formal complaint to the Federal Trade Commission and also shall be used as evidence in pending litigation provided you fail to comply with this offer of settlement.

Despite my three written requests, the unverified items listed below still remain on my credit report in violation of Federal Law. In the results of your investigations, you stated in writing that you **"verified"** that these items are being **"reported correctly"?** Who verified these accounts? How did they verify them? You still have not provided me with the name of the individual, business address, and telephone number of the person or business contacted during your re-investigation. You have **NOT** provided me a copy of ANY original documentation (a consumer contract with my signature on it. Furthermore, you have failed to provide the method of verification as required under **Section 611 (a) (7)**.   Please be advised that under **Section 611 (5)(A)** of the FCRA – you are required to *"…promptly DELETE all information which cannot be verified."*

The law is very clear as to the Civil liability and the remedy available to me (**Section 616 & 617**) if you fail to comply with Federal Law. I am a litigious consumer and fully intend on pursuing litigation in this matter to enforce my rights under the FCRA.

In order to avoid legal action, I demand that you send me copies of the documents you used to verify the following accounts listed below or you delete them immediately. Please provide me with a copy of an updated and corrected credit report showing that these items have been deleted.

Name of Account:	Account Number:	Provide Physical Proof of Verification
1. Chase Bank	#533376304023 ...	Unverified Account

(Hand Write this information with blue ink pen)

Note: If they have already removed some of the items that you listed on your first & second letter than remove them from your list on this letter.

Thank you,

Your Signature Here

Your Name Here

_____

[signature of affiant]

John Doe
2222 Brook Meade St.
Memphis, TN 38127

Subscribed and sworn to before me, this 30th day of April, 2012.

NOTARY SEAL:

_____

[signature of Notary]

_____

[print name of Notary]

NOTARY PUBLIC

My commission expires:
_____, 20_____.

Attached: Copy of my Social Security Card & Driver's License is attached

Sent: USPS Certified Mail

```
┌──────────────────────────────────────┐
│                                      │
│                                      │
│         COPY of SSN CARD             │
│                                      │
│                                      │
└──────────────────────────────────────┘
```

```
┌──────────────────────────────────────┐
│                                      │
│                                      │
│          COPY OF ID CARD             │
│                                      │
│                                      │
└──────────────────────────────────────┘
```

Over time, if you have to file a complaint with the FTC and/ or your State Attorney General, you will have a strong supported case against the Credit Bureau and this evidence will be invaluable should you ever have to go to the unusual extreme of filing a lawsuit to seek damages.

IMPORTANT: Every time you send one of the letters to the credit bureau, make sure that you include a copy of your driver's license and SS card. Remember, we told you to go to your copy center and make 12 or 15 copies so you have them handy to attach to each letter you mail out. If you fail to attach a copy of these documents to each letter you will probably get a reply after waiting 21-30 days that simply tells you that they are unable to respond to your request because there was no proof of who you are attached to the dispute letter. It's another delay tactic that they use to discourage you and it just delays things for you.

After they receive your first dispute letter the Credit Bureaus have 30 days to investigate your dispute and send you a reply. In most cases, they will send you an "acknowledgement letter" that appear to state that they will not investigate your dispute and/or they will tell you that you are illegally trying to dispute legitimate items on your credit report and they may ask you to fill out a form or questionnaire and return it to them. DO NOT FILL OUT ANY FORMS and return it to them. Simply respond to them with the next letter that we have for you in this package.

NOTE: Sometimes the credit bureaus will remove only 2 or 3 of the items and leave 4 or 5 of them still on your report after your first or second letter. If this happens, just continue on with the next letter that you send them but make sure that you don't list the "removed" accounts on the next letter.

GLOSSARY

Acceleration: To speed up; to bring future obligations current.

Acceleration Clause: The part of a contract that says when a loan may be declared due and payable.

Accidental Death Benefit: In a life insurance policy, benefit in addition to the death benefit paid to the beneficiary, should death occur due to an accident. There can be certain exclusions as well as time and age limits.

Account Classification: A system used by reporting agencies to identify which type of account the consumer opened. For example, revolving account, installment loan, or mortgage.

Account Rating: A term used by creditors to refer to the relative status of your account. Each creditor might have its own internal rating system.

Account Number: A unique number given to a person. Your account number is the same as the credit card number.

Acquiring Financial Institution: Merchants must maintain an account with an acquiring financial institution to receive credit for credit card transactions. Daily credit card totals are deposited into the merchant's account minus any fees.

Active Participant: Person whose absence from a planned event would trigger a benefit if the event needs to be canceled or postponed.

Activities of Daily Living: Bathing, preparing and eating meals, moving from room to room, getting into and out of beds or chairs, dressing, using a toilet.

Actual Cash Value: Cost of replacing damaged or destroyed property with comparable new property, minus depreciation and obsolescence. For example, a 10-year-old sofa will not be replaced at current full value because of a decade of depreciation.

Actuary: A specialist in the mathematics of insurance who calculates rates, reserves, dividends and other statistics. (Americanism: In most other countries the individual is known as "mathematician.")

Add-On Interest: Interest that is computed at the beginning of the loan, then added to the principal, so that all must be repaid, even if the loan is paid off early.

Additional Card Holder: Allows you to add a family member to your credit card. They have access to the same credit limit and interest rate that you do.

Additional Principal Payment: Extra money included with a loan payment to pay off the amount owed faster. Over time, this practice reduces the amount of interest paid.

Adjudication: The act of a court of law making an order or judgment.

Adjustable Rate: An interest rate that changes based on changes in a published market-rate index.

Adjudication: The act of a court of law making an order or judgment.

Adjustable Rate: An interest rate that changes based on changes in a published market-rate index.

Adjusted Balances: A method used by some card issuers in whom they subtract all payments made during the month, and then add the finance charges.

Adjuster: A representative of the insurer who seeks to determine the extent of the insurer's liability for loss when a claim is submitted.

Admitted Assets: Assets permitted by state law to be included in an insurance company's annual statement. These assets are an important factor when regulators measure insurance company solvency. They include mortgages, stocks, bonds and real estate.

Affidavit: A sworn, written declaration, usually signed before a notary public.

Affinity Card: A card offered by two organizations, one a lending institution, the other a non-financial group. Schools, nonprofit groups, pro wrestlers, popular singers and airlines are among those featured on affinity cards. Usually, use of the card entitles holders to special discounts or deals from the non-financial group.

Agent: An individual who sells and services insurance policies in either of two classifications:

1. Independent agent represents at least two insurance companies and (at least in theory) services clients by searching the market for the most advantageous price for the most coverage. The agent's commission is a percentage of each premium paid and includes a fee for servicing the insured's policy.

2. Direct or career agent represents only one company and sells only its policies. This agent is paid on a commission basis in much the same manner as the independent agent.

Agent Banks: Smaller banks that serve as agents for larger banks in credit card services.

Aggregate Limit: Usually refers to liability insurance and indicates the amount of coverage that the insured has under the contract for a specific period of time, usually the contract period, no matter how many separate accidents might occur.

Air Miles: One of the most popular rewards issued by airline affiliated co-branded cards. Air miles are earned with every use of the card, and then transferred monthly to the cardholder's account with that airline.

Amount Financed: The principal that is financed. It could include the cost of the purchase and other items rolled into the payments.

Annual Administrative Fee: Charge for expenses associated with administering a group employee benefit plan.

Annual Crediting Cap: The maximum rate that the equity-indexed annuity can be credited in a year. If a contract has an upper limit, or cap, of 7 percent and the index linked to the annuity gained 7.2 percent, only 7 percent would be credited to the annuity.

Annual Fee: A bank charge for use of a credit card levied each year, which can range from $15 to $300 dollars, billed directly to the customer's monthly statement. Many credit cards come without an annual fee.

Annual Percentage Rate (APR): A yearly rate of interest that includes fees and costs paid to acquire the loan. Lenders are required by law to disclose the APR. The rate is calculated in a standard way, taking the average compound interest rate over the term of the loan, so borrowers can compare loans. In mortgages, it is the interest rate of a mortgage when taking into account the interest, mortgage insurance, and certain closing costs including points paid at closing. There is no APR in an automobile lease. Instead, the cost of money is expressed as the money factor.

Annuitization Options: Choices in the way to annuitize. For example, life with a 10-year period certain means payout will last a lifetime, but should the annuitant die during the first 10 years, the payments will continue to beneficiaries through the 10th year. Selection of such an option reduces the amount of the periodic payment.

Annuity: An agreement by an insurer to make periodic payments that continue during the survival of the annuitant(s) or for a specified period.

Application: A document in which a prospective borrower details his or her financial situation to qualify for a loan.

Application Fee: What the lender charges to process the document in which a prospective borrower details his or her financial situation to qualify for a loan.

Approved for Reinsurance: Indicates the company is approved (or authorized) to write reinsurance on risks in this state. A license to write reinsurance might not be required in these states.

Approved or Not Disapproved for Surplus Lines: Indicates the company is approved (or not disapproved) to write excess or surplus lines in this state.

APR: Annual Percentage Rate: A yearly rate of interest that includes fees and costs paid to acquire the loan. Lenders are required by law to disclose the APR. The rate is calculated in a standard way, taking the average compound interest rate over the term of the loan, so borrowers can compare loans.

ATM: An acronym for Automated Teller Machine. It's a terminal activated by a magnetically encoded card that allows customers of a bank or other financial institution to conduct certain transactions such as deposits and withdrawals. An interconnection of these terminals allows customers to conduct certain transactions around the nation and the world, usually subject to a surcharge fee.

Asset: Anything you own that has value and could be turned into cash.

Asset Case: A bankruptcy proceeding in which there are non: exempt assets that might be available to pay the claims of creditors.

Assignment (of wages or other property): To transfer an interest in certain property to another.

ATM Access Fee: Fee charged in addition to the individual account fees for an account holder to gain access to the ATM system. Can be monthly, weekly, or annual fee.

Attained Age: Insured's age at a particular time. For example, many term life insurance policies allow an insured to convert to permanent insurance without a physical examination at the insured's then attained age. Upon conversion, the premium usually rises substantially to reflect the insured's age and diminished life expectancy.

Audit: An official examination of accounts and records.

Authorized Under Federal Products Liability Risk Retention Act (Risk Retention Groups): Indicates companies operating under the Federal Products Liability Risk Retention Act of 1981 and the Liability Risk Retention Act of 1986.

Authorized User: Any person to whom you give permission to use a credit card account.

Automatic Payment: An arrangement that authorizes periodic withdrawals to be made from a checking or savings account to pay bills, usually regular monthly payments such as for rent or mortgages.

Automatic Stay: An injunction that stops lawsuits, foreclosure, garnishments and all collection activity against the debtor the moment a bankruptcy petition is filed.

Automatic Transfer: An arrangement that moves money at certain specified times, often monthly, from an interest: bearing or savings account into a non: interest, usually checking account for the payment of checks or other drafts.

Automobile Liability Insurance: Coverage if an insured is legally liable for bodily injury or property damage caused by an automobile.

Average Daily Balance: This is the method by which most credit cards calculate your payment due. An average daily balance is determined by adding each day's balance and then dividing that total by the number of days in a billing cycle.

Bad Debt: An outstanding balance that has been called due by the creditor and has not been paid.

Balance : The amount of money on a credit card that a person has left to repay.

Balance Sheet: An accounting term referring to a listing of a company's assets, liabilities and surplus as of a specific date.

Balance Transfer: The process of moving an unpaid credit card debt from one issuer to another. Card issuers sometimes offer teaser rates to encourage balance transfers coming in and balance transfer fees to discourage them from going out.

Balance Transfer Fee: Fee charged to customers for transferring an outstanding balance from one card to another.

Bank: An institution that acts as a financial intermediary by receiving money from depositors and lender and also lending to borrowers. A bank must be chartered and meet certain criteria. Chartering is done by the Comptroller of the Currency for national banks, by the Federal Reserve System for state member banks, by the Federal Deposit Insurance Corporation (FDIC) for insured banks, and by state regulatory agencies. Also referred to as a commercial bank.

Bank Card System: Credit card networks that allow smaller institutions to offer credit card products even though they could not support all the services needed by themselves.

Bank Holding Company: A company that owns or controls one or more banks or companies associated with banking such as leasing companies, credit companies, etc. It is usually identified by the word Bancorp or Bancshares in the name. The Federal Reserve Board of Governors regulates all bank holding companies.

Bankruptcy: Legal process in the federal court system that gives debtors protection from asset seizure when debts are in default. The court takes possession of the assets remaining and distributes them equitably among the creditors. Repayment of debt is handled through the court trustees.

Bankruptcy Code: The informal name for Title 11 of the United States Code (11 U.S.C. & 101: 1330), the federal bankruptcy law.

Bankruptcy Trustee: A private individual or corporation appointed in all Chapter 7, Chapter 12, and Chapter 13 cases to represent the interests of the bankruptcy estate and the debtor's creditors.

Basis Point: One one-hundredth of a percentage point. The difference between 8.04 percent and 8.05 percent is one basis point.

Beneficiary: Person designated to receive funds or other property from an estate or trust.

Benefit Period: In health insurance, the number of days for which benefits are paid to the named insured and his or her dependents. For example, the number of days that benefits are calculated for a calendar year consists of the days beginning on Jan. 1 and ending on Dec. 31 of each year.

Best's Capital Adequacy Relativity (BCAR): This percentage measures a company's relative capital strength compared to its industry peer composite. A company's BCAR, which is an important component in determining the appropriateness of its rating, is calculated by dividing a company's capital adequacy ratio by the capital adequacy ratio of the median of its industry peer composite using Best's proprietary capital mode. Capital adequacy ratios are calculated as the net required capital necessary to support components of underwriting, asset, and credit risks in relation to economic surplus.

Bill Presentment: An online system that allows customers to receive and view the bill on a computer, and then pay the bill electronically. Users can pay their bills immediately and the money is transferred from the account.

Billing Cycle: The number of days between the last statement date and the current statement date.

Billing Statement: The monthly bill sent by a credit card issuer to the customer. It gives activity on an account, including balance, purchases, payments, credits and finance charges. Important changes to a credit card account are often included in small print fliers that are sent with the statement.

Bond: A written promise of another (surety) to pay a debt in the event the debtor fails to pay.

Borrower: One who gets a loan.

Broker: Insurance salesperson that searches the marketplace in the interest of clients, not insurance companies.

Broker-Agent: Independent insurance salesperson that represents particular insurers but also might function as a broker by searching the entire insurance market to place an applicant's coverage to maximize protection and minimize cost. This person is licensed as an agent and a broker.

Business Net Retention: This item represents the percentage of a company's gross writings that are retained for its own account. Gross writings are the sum of direct writings and assumed writings. This measure excludes affiliated writings.

Cancellation Clause: A provision in a lease or other contract that spells out under what conditions the parties can call off the deal.

Capital: Equity of shareholders of a stock insurance company. The company's capital and surplus are measured by the difference between its assets minus its liabilities. This value protects the interests of the company's policy owners in the event it develops financial problems; the policy owners' benefits are thus protected by the insurance company's capital. Shareholders' interest is second to that of policy owners.

Capitalization or Leverage: Measures the exposure of a company's surplus to various operating and financial practices. A highly leveraged, or poorly capitalized, company can show a high return on surplus, but might be exposed to a high risk of instability.

Captive Agent: Representative of a single insurer or fleet of insurers who is obliged to submit business only to that company, or at the very minimum, give that company first refusal rights on a sale. In exchange, that insurer usually provides its captive agents with an allowance for office expenses as well as an extensive list of employee benefits such as pensions, life insurance, health insurance, and credit unions.

Card Holder Agreement: The written statement that gives the terms and conditions of a credit card account. The cardholder agreement is required by Federal Reserve regulations. It must include the Annual Percentage Rate, the monthly minimum payment formula, annual fee, if applicable, and the cardholder's rights in billing disputes. Changes in the cardholder agreement may be made, with written advance notice, at any time by the issuer. Rules for imposing changes vary from state to state, but the rules that apply are those of the home state of the issuing bank, not the home state of the cardholder. See national issuers.

Case Management: A system of coordinating medical services to treat a patient, improve care and reduce cost. A case manager coordinates health care delivery for patients.

Cash Advance: An instant loan from a credit card company. The advance is charged interest the day it was required until it is paid off. A cash advance usually has a higher interest rate that regular purchases and some credit card companies charge a transaction fee.

Cash Advance Fee: A charge by the bank for using credit cards to obtain cash. This fee can be stated in terms of a flat per-transaction fee or a percentage of the amount of the cash advance. For example, the fee may be expressed as follows:"2%/$10". This means that the cash advance fee will be the greater of 2% of the cash advance amount or $10. The banks may limit the amount that can be charged to a specific dollar amount. Depending on the bank issuing the card, the cash advance fee may be deducted directly from the cash advance at the time the money is received or it may be posted to your bill as of the day you received the advance. The cost of a cash advance is also higher because there generally is no grace period. Interest accrues from the moment the money is withdrawn.

Cash Advance Rate: When banks allow credit cardholders to borrow cash, they often charge a higher rate of interest than they do for purchases. Usually, banks also charge a fee for each cash advance, and the interest accrues from the moment the money is withdrawn.

Cash Back: A credit card company pays a card holder a percentage of the purchases they make usually between .05% to 5%.

Casualty: Liability or loss resulting from an accident.

Casualty Insurance: That type of insurance that is primarily concerned with losses caused by injuries to persons and legal liability imposed upon the insured for such injury or for damage to property of others. It also includes such diverse forms as plate glass, insurance against crime, such as robbery, burglary and forgery, boiler and machinery insurance and Aviation insurance. Many casualty companies also write surety business.

Ceded Reinsurance Leverage: The ratio of the reinsurance premiums ceded, plus net ceded reinsurance balances from non-US affiliates for paid losses, unpaid losses, incurred but not reported (IBNR), unearned premiums and commissions, fewer funds held from reinsurers, plus ceded reinsurance balances payable, to policyholders' surplus. This ratio measures the company's dependence upon the security provided by its reinsurers and its potential exposure to adjustment on such reinsurance.

Change in Net Premiums Written (IRIS): The annual percentage change in Net Premiums Written. A company should demonstrate its ability to support controlled business growth with quality surplus growth from strong internal capital generation.

Change in Policyholder Surplus (IRIS): The percentage change in policyholder surplus from the prior year-end derived from operating earnings, investment gains, net contributed capital and other miscellaneous sources. This ratio measures a company's ability to increase policyholders' security.

Chargeback: A customer disputes a charge on their credit card, and the credit card company removes the charge from the customer's bill and charges the merchant for the purchase.

Chartered Property and Casualty Underwriter (CPCU): Professional designation earned after the successful completion of 10 national examinations given by the American Institute for Property and Liability Underwriters.

Cover such areas of expertise as insurance, risk management, economics, finance, management, accounting, and law. Three Years of work experience also are required in the insurance business or a related area.

Cash Cards: Cash cards, often called gift cards, are similar to prepaid phone cards and contain a set amount of value, which can be read by a special cash card reader. Participating retailers will use the reader to debit the card in increments until the value is gone. The cards are like cash, they have no built-in security, and so, if lost or stolen, they can be used by anyone.

Caveat: A warning or caution.

Caveat Emptor: Latin for "let the buyer beware." It means that the buyer of a property or item buys it at his or her own risk.

Chapter 11: A reorganization bankruptcy, usually involving a corporation or partnership. (A Chapter 11 debtor usually proposes a plan of reorganization to keep its business alive and pay creditors over time. People in business or individuals can also seek relief in Chapter 11.)

Chapter 12: Chapter of the Bankruptcy Code designed to give special relief to a family farmer with regular income.

Chapter 13: The chapter of the Bankruptcy Code providing for adjustment of debts of an individual with regular income. (Chapter 13 allows a debtor to keep property and pay debts over time, usually three to five years.)

Chapter 7: The chapter of the Bankruptcy Code providing for liquidation. The sale of a debtor's nonexempt property and the distribution of the proceeds to creditors.

Charge Card: A card that requires a full payment of the charge by the due date. Unlike credit cards, which give borrowers a revolving line of credit and lets them borrow against it, carrying a balance with an agreed to interest rate, charge cards do not allow carrying a balance and no interest is charged. American Express and Diner's Club are examples of charge cards.

Charge Off: Action taken by a creditor that declares a debt uncollectable and allows that creditor to expense the balance as a loss for business and tax purposes.

Civil Judgment: Decision by a court that a debt is owed and an order is issued to pay the debt to the creditor, enforceable by certain actions, such as garnishment of assets and wages in some states.

Civil Remedies: The legal means of enforcing a civil (as opposed to criminal) right.

Claim: Filing by a creditor in a bankruptcy case that states money owed by the debtor.

Class 3-6 Bonds (% of PHS): This test measures exposure to noninvestment grade bonds as a percentage of surplus. Generally, noninvestment grade bonds carry higher default and illiquidity risks. The designation of quality classifications that coincide with different bond ratings assigned by major credit rating agencies.

Classic Card: Brand name for the standard card issued by VISA.

Closed-Account Fee: A fee charged for shutting down an account. Sometimes charged if the account is closed before a certain time period has passed.

Closed-End Credit: An agreement in which the borrower agrees to pay the loan plus any finance charges in full over a definite period. It usually applies to real estate and automobile loans.

CM: Short for compounding method. Used in Bank Rate tables. These include: S: Simple interest. A: Compounded annually. H: Compounded monthly. D: Compounded daily.

CO-Branded Cards: This term has two uses in the credit card industry. 1) A type of affinity card issued through a partnership between a bank and another retail company. For instance, a large department store may co-brand a card with a bank. The card would have two brand names on it, the bank's name and the store's name. Usually, the attraction of the card is rewards from the retail partner, such as airlines. 2) A credit or debit card that carries the logo of one of the major credit card issuers such as American Express, Discover, MasterCard or Visa.

Co-Signer: A person who signs a promissory note that is also signed by one or more other parties. All parties take responsibility for the debt if any of the others renege.

COFI: Short for cost of funds index. A yield index based upon the cost of funds to savings & loan institutions in the San Francisco Federal Home Loan Bank District. It is one of the indexes commonly used to set the rate of adjustable rate mortgages.

Coinsurance: In property insurance, requires the policyholder to carry insurance equal to a specified percentage of the value of property to receive full payment on a loss. For health insurance, it is a percentage of each claim above the deductible paid by the policyholder. For a 20% health insurance coinsurance clause, the policyholder pays for the deductible plus 20% of his covered losses. After paying 80% of losses up to a specified ceiling, the insurer starts paying 100% of losses.

Collateral: Asset pledged to back a debt when the debt is incurred. It can be seized if the debtor defaults.

Collection: Term commonly used by creditors to mean in default and actively pursued for payment.

Collection Agency: Company that contracts with creditors to pursue collection activities when a debt is not paid on time. A collection agency can also purchase the debt from the original creditor for a discount and collect the money for itself.

Collision Insurance: Covers physical damage to the insured's automobile (other than that covered under comprehensive insurance) resulting from contact with another inanimate object.

Combined Ratio After Policyholder Dividends: The sum of the loss, expense and policyholder dividend ratios not reflecting investment income or income taxes. This ratio measures the company's overall underwriting profitability, and a combined ratio of less than 100 indicates an underwriting profit.

Commercial Bank: A financial institution that provides a broad range of services, from checking and savings accounts to business loans and credit cards.

Commercial Lines: Refers to insurance for businesses, professionals and commercial establishments.

Commission: Fee paid to an agent or insurance salesperson as a percentage of the policy premium. The percentage varies widely depending on coverage, the insurer and the marketing methods.

Common Carrier: A business or agency that is available to the public for transportation of persons, goods or messages. Common carriers include trucking companies, bus lines and airlines.

Community Property: Nine states: Arizona, California, Idaho, Louisiana, Nevada, New Mexico, Texas, Washington and Wisconsin are community property states. In those states community property includes real estate, tangible assets, and the earnings of both spouses acquired during the marriage. Assets acquired by gift or inheritance or assets owned before the marriage is not community property.

Complaint: The first document filed in a civil lawsuit.

Compliance: Acting in accordance with certain legal requirements.

Compounding Method: Used in bank rate tables. These include: S: Simple interest. A: Compounded annually. H: Compounded semi-annually. Q: Compounded quarterly. M: Compounded monthly. D: Compounded daily.

Comprehensive Insurance: Auto insurance coverage providing protection in the event of physical damage (other than collision) or theft of the insured car. For example, fire damage or a cracked windshield would be covered under the comprehensive section.

Comptroller of the Currency: An officer of the Treasury Department who is responsible for chartering national banks and has primary supervisory authority over them.

Concurrent Periods: In hospital income protection, when a patient is confined to a hospital due to more than one injury and/or illness at the same time, benefits are paid as if the total disability resulted from only one cause.

Conditional Reserves: This item represents the aggregate of various reserves which, for technical reasons, are treated by companies as liabilities. Such reserves, which are similar to free resources or surplus, include unauthorized reinsurance, excess of statutory loss reserves over statement reserves, dividends to policyholders undeclared and other similar reserves established voluntarily or in compliance with statutory regulations.

Consolidation: Act of combining two or more debts into one.

Consolidation Loan: Loan that combines and refinances other loans or debt. It is normally an installment loan designed to reduce the dollar amount of an individual's monthly payments.

Consumer: Usually an individual who purchases and/or uses goods and services.

Consumer Credit: Loans for personal or household use as opposed to business or commercial lending. Loans are generally unsecured, not backed by collateral.

Consumer Credit Counseling Service: A service that offers counseling about how to work out a realistic budget and debt repayment plan and work with creditors. The goal is to ensure that debts are paid back over time.

Consumer Credit Protection Act: The Consumer Credit Protection Act, passed in 1968, for the first time spelled out basic consumer protections, including Truth in Lending disclosures. It requires creditors to state the cost of borrowing in understandable terms to allow consumers to figure out how much loans would cost, and to compare them.

Consumer Debts: Debts incurred for personal, as opposed to business, needs.

Consumer File: Record of all the credit histories collected by a credit reporting agency.

Consumer Lease: A lease or rental agreement, typically for a vehicle or household goods, between a business and an individual.

Consumer Price Index: Also known as CPI. A measure of the cost of living determined by the Bureau of Labor Statistics.

Consumer Report: Report summarizing the information held in the consumer file at a credit reporting agency.

Consumer Statement: Written statement placed on a credit report disputing or explaining circumstances surrounding a credit reference on the report.

Contingent Liability: A liability that does not become effective until another acts or fails to act in accordance with an agreement.

Contract: In real estate parlance, the contract is the legal document by which buyer and seller make offers and counteroffers. The real estate contract describes the property, includes or excludes items in the property, names the price, apportions the closing costs between the parties and sets forth a closing date. When buyer and seller agree on terms and sign the same document, the property is said to be "under contract." More formally known as agreement for sale, purchase agreement or earnest money contract.

Convertible: Term life insurance coverage that can be converted into permanent insurance regardless of an insured's physical condition and without a medical examination. The individual cannot be denied coverage or charged an additional premium for any health problems.

Copayment: A predetermined, flat fee an individual pay for health-care services, in addition to what insurance covers. For example, some HMOs require a $10 copayment for each office visit, regardless of the type or level of services provided during the visit. Copayments are not usually specified by percentages.

Co-Signer: Person who is contractually obligated to back a debt if the original signer is unable to pay.

Cost of Funds Index: A yield index based upon the cost of funds to savings & loan institutions in the San Francisco Federal Home Loan Bank District. It is one of the indexes commonly used to set the rate of adjustable rate mortgages.

Cost-of-Living Adjustment (COLA): Automatic adjustment applied to Social Security retirement payments when the consumer price index increases at a rate of at least 3%, the first quarter of one year to the first quarter of the next year.

Counterclaim: A claim filed by an individual against whom a first claim has already been filed by another individual or business.

Coverage: The scope of protection provided under an insurance policy. In property insurance, coverage lists perils insured against, properties covered, locations covered, individuals insured, and the limits of indemnification. In life insurance, living and death benefits are listed.

Coverage Area: The geographic region covered by travel insurance.

Credit: Money that a lender gives to a borrower on condition of repayment over a certain period.

Credit Analysis: Process used by a creditor to decide which consumers to grant credit.

Credit Balance: Amount of money a bank owes to a customer. This can happen when you buy something   and return it. The merchant then credits your card the price.

Credit Bureau: A company that collects and sells information about how people handle credit. It issues credit reports that list how individuals manage their debts and make payments, how much untapped credit they have available and whether they have applied for any loans. The reports are made available to individuals and to creditors who profess to have a legitimate need for the information. The three major national credit bureaus are Equifax, Experian (formerly TRW) and TransUnion. Often called credit reporting agency.

Credit Bureau Members/Subscribers: Businesses that pay a fee to belong to or do business with the credit bureaus and therefore, are able to order the reports they produce.

Credit Capacity: Amount of credit that a creditor determines a consumer can handle, given income and other obligations.

Credit Card: A plastic card with a coded magnetic stripe that, when signed, entities its bearer to a revolving line of credit, with a credit limit and interest rate determined by the borrower's income and credit report. Credit cards began in the late "40's when banks began giving out paper certificates that could be used like cash in local stores. The first real credit card was issued in 1951 by Franklin National Bank in New York.

Credit Card Number: An exclusive number assigned to each card.

Credit Freeze: Also known as a security freeze, a credit freeze is essentially a lockdown on your credit report and score. It blocks new lenders from accessing your credit file without your permission. Since most credit issuers require a credit check before granting credit, the credit freeze should block most unauthorized attempts to obtain new credit in your name.

Credit Grantor: Individual or business that extends a consumer/debtor a loan or line of credit.

Credit History: A record of a person's use of credit overtime, reflecting how much was borrowed, whether payments were on time, and how much is still owed.

Credit Insurance: A policy that pays off the card debt should the borrower lose his job, die or become disabled. The structure of protection for a revolving credit card debt is calculated each month to cover only the debt that existed at the last billing cycle.

Credit Life Insurance: A type of life insurance that helps repay the loan if the consumer become disabled. It is optional coverage. When taken out, the cost of the policy is sometimes rolled into the loan principal amount.

Credit Limit: The maximum amount of charges a cardholder may apply to the account. The Consumer Federation of America suggests people carry credit lines no greater than 20% percent of their gross household income. For example, people with a gross income of $50,000 would cap credit lines at $10,000.

Credit Line: The maximum amount of money available in an open-end credit arrangement such as credit card, or overdraft protection.

Credit Monitoring Service: A commercial service that alerts consumers of significant changes in their credit file for a fee. Features and prices vary by service provider.

Credit Rating: A judgment of someone's ability to repay debts, based on current and projected income and history of payment of past debts. Sometimes expressed as a number called a credit score.

Credit Reference: Individual or business that has loaned consumer money and is reporting to a credit bureau the experience on that account.

Credit Report: A document containing financial information about a person, focusing on his or her history of paying obligations, such as a mortgage, car payment, utilities, and credit cards. Also includes current balances on outstanding debts, the individual's amount of available credit, public records such as bankruptcies, and inquiries about credit from various companies. A person with a good credit report is likely to get a better interest rate than someone with a poor credit report.

Credit Reporting Agency: A company that collects and sells Information about how people handle credit. It issues credit reports that list how individuals manage their debts and make payments, how much untapped credit they have available and whether they have applied for any loans. The reports are made available to individuals and to creditors who profess to have a legitimate need for the information. The three major national credit bureaus are Equifax, Experian and TransUnion.

Credit Repository: An antiquated term for a credit bureau.

Credit Score: A three-digit number that reflects the credit history detailed by a person's credit report. Lenders calculate this number with the assistance of computer systems as part of the process of assigning rates and terms to the loans they make. The higher the number, the better the terms that a lender will offer. Credit scores are also increasingly used by others in making decisions about whether to do business with a consumer, and on what terms. For example, many auto insurance companies increase the insurance premium for people with low credit scores, in the belief that there is a relationship between credit score and making insurance claims.

Credit Scoring System: A numerical system designed to measure the likelihood that a borrower will repay a debt created by assigning scores to various characteristics connected to creditworthiness.

Credit Union: A non-profit cooperative financial institution owned and controlled by the people who use its services, usually a group such as employees in the same company or industry. Credit unions historically have been able to offer lower rates and fees and still operate in the black. Credit unions rely on a financial reserve to absorb unexpected losses from loan defaults or other financial setbacks, and the majority of credit unions carry federal deposit insurance that protects individual accounts up to a specified amount in the event the credit union fails.

Creditor: One who is owed money.

Creditor Meeting: ("341 meeting") The meeting that takes place three to six weeks after the bankruptcy petition is filed, at which time the debtor may be questioned by the court appointed trustee and the debtors" creditors about the information provided by the debtor on the bankruptcy petition.

Creditable Coverage: Term means that benefits provided by other drug plans are at least as good as those provided by the new Medicare Part D program. This may be important to people eligible for Medicare Part D but who do not sign up at their first opportunity because if the other plans provide creditable coverage, plan members can later convert to Medicare Part D without paying higher premiums than those in effect during their open enrollment period.

Current Liquidity (IRIS): The sum of cash, unaffiliated invested assets and encumbrances on other properties to net liabilities plus ceded reinsurance balances payable, expressed as a percent. This ratio measures the proportion of liabilities covered by unencumbered cash and unaffiliated investments. If this ratio is less than 100, the company's solvency is dependent on the collectability or marketability of premium balances and investments in affiliates. This ratio assumes the collectability of all amounts recoverable from reinsurers on paid and unpaid losses and unearned premiums.

Customer Identification File (CIF): A computerized central file of information about a bank's customers that includes account and credit information.

Damages: The estimate money equivalent of an injury or wrong.

Deadbeat List: List of those who owe money but have failed to pay.

Death Benefit: The limit of insurance or the amount of benefit that will be paid in the event of the death of a covered person.

Debit Card: A payment card that is linked directly to a customer's bank account. Some cards require a personal identification number. Others require a customer's signature. A PIN-based or direct debit card removes a purchase price from a customer's checking account almost immediately. A signature based or deferred debit card has a Visa or MasterCard logo and remove the purchase price from a customer's bank account in two or three days.

Debt: Money one person or firm owes to another person or firm.

Debt Consolidation: The replacement of multiple loans with a single loan, often with a lower monthly payment and a longer repayment period. It's also called a consolidation loan.

Debt-To-Income Ratio: The percentage of before tax earnings that are spent to pay off loans for obligations such as auto loans, student loans and credit card balances. Lenders look at two ratios. The front-end ratio is the percentage of monthly before tax earnings that are spent on house payments (including principal, interest, taxes and insurance). In the back-end ratio, the borrower's other debts are factored in.

Debtor: Technically, a person who has filed a petition for relief under the bankruptcy laws. More generally, anyone who owes.

Deductible: Amount of loss that the insured pays before the insurance kicks in.

Deed of Trust: Similar to a mortgage, title to property held by a trustee until a debt affecting real property is paid in full.

Default-1: The condition that occurs when a consumer fails to fulfill the obligations set out in a loan or lease. 2. A designation on a credit report that indicates a person has not paid a debt that was owed. Accounts usually are listed as being in default after several reports of delinquency. Defaults are a serious negative item on a credit report.

Defaulted Account: A credit card account when the customer has not kept their end of the agreement to the contract. A record of defaulted accounts is kept for six years after the customer breaks the agreement.

Deferment: Postponement, particularly of collecting a debt.

Deficiency: The amount by which a creditor's claim is not satisfied and the notice thereof to the debtor.

Delinquent: When an account is not paid per the contractual agreement. It is reported as delinquent on a credit report.

Delinquent Account: A customer fails to repay any of their balance in three months, or a customer has been late on a payment for three months in a year.

Deposition: Statement taken under oath that is to be used in court proceedings.

Developed to Net Premiums Earned: The ratio of developed premiums through the year to net premiums earned. If premium growth was relatively steady, and the mix of business by line didn't materially change, this ratio measures whether or not a company's loss reserves are keeping pace with premium growth.

Development to Policyholder Surplus (IRIS): The ratio measures reserve deficiency or redundancy in relation to policyholder surplus. This ratio reflects the degree to which year-end surplus was either overstated (+) or understated (—) in each of the past several years, if original reserves had been restated to reflect subsequent development through year end.

Digital Wallet: Encryption software that conducts secure transactions online in a fashion that resembles using a physical wallet.

Ding: Indicator on a credit report that some or all companies looking at the report might find negative.

Direct Premiums Written: The aggregate amount of recorded originated premiums, other than reinsurance, written during the year, whether collected or not, at the close of the year, plus retrospective audit premium collections, after deducting all return premiums.

Direct Writer: An insurer whose distribution mechanism is either the direct selling system or the exclusive agency system.

Discharge: Act of releasing the debtor of the obligation of a debt by the bankruptcy court.

Disclosure: The act of revealing certain information, particularly to a debtor regarding his loan.

Discount Rate: The interest rate at which financial institutions that are members of the Federal Reserve System(Fed) may borrow on a short-term basis directly to cover temporary deficiencies in the bank's reserves. Banks borrow from the Fed as a last resort because frequent borrowing would raise concern by bank regulators.

Disease Management: A system of coordinated health-care interventions and communications for patients with certain illnesses.

Dishonored Check: Payment has been denied to the person trying to cash the check.

Dividend: The return of part of the policy's premium for a policy issued on a participating basis by either a mutual or stock insurer. A portion of the surplus paid to the stockholders of a corporation.

Double Cycle Billing: A credit card practice where the consumer is charged interest on debt already paid. Here's how it works: A cardholder begins a billing cycle with a zero balance and charges $500 on a credit card. They make an on-time payment of $450. With double-cycle billing, they would be charged interest on the $500, instead of the $50 still owed in the next billing cycle.

Down Payment: An initial, partial payment on a purchase. This payment is typically a small portion of the total purchase price, and reduces the amount of the purchase that must be financed. When buying a home or automobile, for example, your down payment might be 5%, 10%, or 20% of the total purchase price.

Earned Premium: The amount of the premium that has been paid for in advance that has been "earned" by virtue of the fact that time has passed without claim. A three-year policy that has been paid in advance and is one year old would have only partly earned the premium.

Economic Hardship: Financially severely difficult.

E-Commerce: A system used to conduct business transactions of buying and selling goods and services over a computer network.

Effective Federal Funds Rate: The average interest rate that federal funds actually trade at in a day. The federal funds rate will remain stable for months at a time, but the effective rate is a volatile one that will vary every business day.

EFT: Electronic funds transfer. The transfer of money between accounts by consumer electronic systems such as automated teller machines (ATMs), and electronic payment of bills.

Electronic Cash: Also known as e-cash. A system used to transfer cash over the internet to pay for goods and service.

Electronic Check Presentment: Called ECP for short, it captures an electronic image of the check at the point of sale. The image, rather than the paper check, is then processed by banks and clearinghouses. The way it works is that a depositing bank sends the paying bank (or a Federal Reserve Bank) an electronic transmission containing the details of a check, such as the amount, account number and check number that the depositing bank will be presenting later in the day or the following business day.

Electronic Commerce: A system used to conduct business transactions of buying and selling goods and services over a computer network.

Electronic Funds Transfer: The transfer of money between accounts by consumer electronic systems such as automated teller machine (ATMs), and electronic payment of bills.

Elimination Period: The time which must pass after filing a claim before policyholder can collect insurance benefits. Also known as "waiting period."

Employers Liability Insurance: Coverage against common law liability of an employer for accidents to employees, as distinguished from liability imposed by a workers' compensation law.

Encryption: A method for ensuring the privacy and security of a consumer's personal finance information at a bank or financial institution Web site. Encryption is the process of scrambling data so that only the intended receiver can use it. To be effective, encryption needs to be used by both the sender and the receiver. Consumers should make sure it is being used when sending sensitive information.

Encumbrance: A claim on property, such as a mortgage, a lien for work and materials, or a right of dower. The interest of the property owner is reduced by the amount of the encumbrance.

Equal Credit Opportunity Act: A federal law that prohibits discrimination in credit transactions on the basis of race, color, religion, national origin, sex, marital status, age, source of income or the exercise of any right under the Consumer Credit Protection Act.

Equifax: One of the three largest credit bureaus, along with Experian and TransUnion.

Equitable Title: The right of ownership, although legal title is held by another.

Equity: The amount of value of property remaining after deducting the mortgage and other pledges or liens rightfully against the property.

Equity Line: A line of credit, or loan, given by a lender with the equity in real estate given as collateral.

Exclusions: Items or conditions that are not covered by the general insurance contract.

Execute: To carry out the terms of a legal document, especially a judgment.

Experian: One of the three largest credit bureaus, along with Equifax and TransUnion.

Expense Ratio: The ratio of underwriting expenses (including commissions) to net premiums written. This ratio measures the company's operational efficiency in underwriting its book of business.

Exposure: Measure of vulnerability to loss, usually expressed in dollars or units.

Express Cash: A special program offered by American Express that allows you to use your credit card at ATM'S

Extended Replacement Cost: This option extends replacement cost loss settlement to personal property and to outdoor antennas, carpeting, domestic appliances, cloth awnings, and outdoor equipment, subject to limitations on certain kinds of personal property; includes inflation protection coverage.

F (Fixed): If the letter "F" appears after the annual percentage rate (APR) the interest rate is fixed and not subject to adjustment.

Fair and Accurate Credit Transaction Act (FACTA): Federal law that expanded the power of the Fair Credit Reporting Act to increase consumer rights.

Fair Credit Billing Act: Passed by Congress in 1975 to help customers resolve billing disputes with card issuers. The act requires issuers to credit payments to a customer's account the day they are received. To be protected under the law, the consumer must write to the issuer within 60 days of the mailing date on the bill with the error. The issuer is then required to investigate and either correct the mistake or explain why the bill is correct within two billing cycles. The issuer also must acknowledge a customer's complaint in writing within 30 days. Each issuer is allowed to set specific payment guidelines. If any of the guidelines are not met, the issuer can take as many as five days to credit the payment.

Fair Credit Reporting Act: A federal law that governs what credit bureaus can report and for how long. It outlines procedures for correcting errors in credit reports. It requires credit bureaus to furnish copies of consumer's credit reports at their request.

Fair Debt Collection Practices Act: A federal law that prohibits certain methods of debt collection, such as harassment.

Fair Market Value: Price at which a willing buyer and willing seller will trade.

FAQ: Short for frequently asked questions. The section of a Web site where the bank or financial institution posts answers to consumers most commonly asked questions about the banking services.

FDIC: Federal Deposit Insurance Corp. An agency of the U.S. government that manages the bank insurance funds, which insure deposits at banks and other qualifying financial institutions up to $250,000 per account ($250,000 on retirement accounts) in interest and principal. FDIC insurance is mandatory for all nationally chartered banks and all banks that are members of the Federal Reserve System. On Oct. 3, 2008, Congress raised the FDIC insurance limit on individual accounts to $250,000 from $100,000. This will remain in effect until Dec. 31,2009, unless it is renewed.

Fed: Congress founded the Federal Reserve, the central bank of the United States, in 1913. It conducts the nation's monetary policy and regulates its banks in order to achieve a flexible and stable economy. The seven members of the Board of Governors of the Federal Reserve System are nominated by the President and confirmed by the Senate to serve 14-year terms. The chairman and the vice chairman of the board are named by the President from among the members and are confirmed by the Senate. They serve a term of four years.

Federal Advisory Council: An advisory group consisting of one member elected from each of the 12 Federal Reserve Districts who meet with the Federal Reserve Board of Governors at least four times each year to make recommendations on business and financial matters.

Federal Deposit Insurance Corporation: An agency of the U.S. government that manages the bank insurance funds, which insure deposits at banks and other, qualifying financial institutions up to $250,000 per account ($250,000 on retirement accounts) in interest and principal. FDIC insurance is mandatory for all nationally chartered banks and all banks that are members of the Federal Reserve System. On Oct. 3, 2008, Congress raised the FDIC insurance limit on individual accounts to $250,000 from $100,000. This will remain in effect until Dec. 31, 2009, unless it is renewed.

Federal Discount Rate: The interest rate at which an eligible financial institution may borrow funds directly from a Federal Reserve Bank. Banks whose reserves dip below the reserve requirement set by the Federal Reserve's board of governors use that money to correct their shortage. The board of directors of each reserve bank sets the discount rate every 14 days. It's considered the last resort for banks, which usually borrow from each other.

Federal Funds Rate: The interest rate at which banks and other depository institutions lend money to each other, usually on an overnight basis. Set by the Federal Reserve Open Market Committee, which meets eight times a year. When you read the headline "Fed change rates," this is the rate that is changed. How it works: The Fed requires banks to keep a certain percentage of their customers' money on reserve, where the banks earn no interest on it. Consequently, Banks try to stay as close to the reserve limit as possible without going under it, lending money back and forth to maintain the proper level. The Fed does not control the federal funds rate directly; instead, it sets a target, which it meets by adding cash to subtracting cash from the Federal Reserve System.

121

Federal Open Market Committee: The 12-member committee meets eight times a year to set guidelines for the Federal Reserve regarding the sale and purchase of government securities in the open market. Its chief importance for consumers is that the FOMC can adjust the federal funds rate and the federal discount rate. Banks set their rates based on the FOMC'S moves, and therefore the committee's actions effectively ratchet consumer interest rates upward or downward. The committee is comprised of the seven members of the Board of Governors. The president of the Federal Reserve Bank of New York, and of the presidents of the other 11 reserve banks.

Federal Reserve Board: Congress founded the Federal Reserve, the central bank of the United States, in 1913. It conducts the nation's monetary policy and regulates its banks in order to achieve a flexible and stable economy. The seven members of the Board of Governors of the Federal Reserve System are nominated by the President and confirmed by the Senate to serve a 14-year term. The chairman and the vice chairman of the board are named by the president from among the members and are confirmed by the Senate. They serve a term of four years.

Federal Reserve Board of Governors: The seven-member governing board of the Federal Reserve System. Members are appointed by the president and confirmed by the Senate for their 14-year terms. The board supervises the activities of the Fed and, as the majority of the Federal Open Market Committee (FOMC), is principally responsible for the conduct of monetary policy.

Federal Reserve System: The central banking system for the United States, known as the "Fed," was established by the Federal Reserve Act of 1913 and serves as the nation's central bank, issuing the nation's currency, conducting monetary policy through the regulation of the money supply and the cost of credit, facilitating the clearing of checks, providing short-term credit to member banks through the discount rate, regulating bank operations, approving interstate bank mergers, supervising bank holding companies, and providing oversight to international banking operations. It includes a seven-member Federal

Reserve Board of Governors, 12 Federal Reserve Districts each with a Federal Reserve Bank (and 24 branch offices), the decision making Federal Open Market Committee(FOMC), AND THE Federal Advisory Council consisting of an elected member from each Federal Reserve District that makes recommendations to the Board of Governors on business and financial matters.

Federal Savings and Loan Insurance Corporation: A federal institution that insures deposits of federally chartered savings and loan associations.

Federal Trade Commission: A federal agency that enforces antitrust and consumer protection laws, including the Truth-in-Lending Act, Fair Credit Billing Act, Fair Credit Reporting Act, Equal Credit Opportunity Act, Fair Debt Collection Practices Act and Home Ownership and Equity Protection Act.

FICO Score (Fair Isaacs): Objective methodology used by credit grantors to determine how much, if any, credit to grant to an applicant. Some factors in scoring are income, assets, length of employment, length of living in one place, and past record of using credit.

Fiduciary: A relationship in which one-person places confidence in another in regard to a particular transaction or one's general affairs or business. The relationship is not necessarily formally or legally established as in a declaration of trust but can be one of moral or personal responsibility.

File and Use Rating Laws: State-based laws which permit insurers to adopt new rates without the prior approval of the insurance department. Usually insurers submit their new rates with supporting statistical data.

File Segregation: Establishment of a new credit identity with inaccurate information.

Finance Charge: The charge for using a credit card, comprised of interest costs and other fees. The finance charge can be calculated with the following formula: Average Daily Balance X Daily Periodic Rate X Number of Days in Billing Cycle.

Financial Statement: A statement, usually requested by a lender, that describes your property, its value, your income and liabilities 9debt), indicating your actual financial condition.

Financing Entity: Provides money for purchases

First Lien: Primary claim by the lender for satisfaction of outstanding debt. A first mortgage creates a first lien.

Five Year Treasury Constant Maturity: An index published by the Federal Reserve Board based on the average yield of a range of Treasury securities, all adjusted to the equivalent of a five-year maturity. Yields on Treasury securities at constant maturity are determined by the U.S. Treasury from the daily yield curve. That is based on the closing market bid yields on actively traded Treasury securities in the over-the-counter market.

Fixed Interest Rate: An interest rate that remains the same even if the prime rate changes. A credit card company can still change a fixed interest rate, but to do so they must tell you they are changing the rate.

Fixed Rate: Set annual percentage rate that does not change in response to interest rate changes and conditions. With credit card accounts, this does not mean that the rate cannot change, only that it will not change automatically with some external index.

Float: The amount of time the bank takes to clear or reject (bounce) a check for payment. The time at which funds are debited from the issuer's account.

Floater: A separate policy available to cover the value of goods beyond the coverage of a standard renter's insurance policy including movable properly such as jewelry or sports equipment.

Floor: The minimum rate possible on a variable rate loan or line of credit, after any initial introductory rate period. For example, on a credit card with the Prime rate as its index, no matter how low the Prime rate drops, the rate on the line may never decrease below the stated rate floor.

FNMA 30 Year Mortgage Commitment Delivery 60 Days: FNMA is the Federal National Mortgage Association, commonly known as Fannie Mae. It purchases Federal Home Administration, Veterans Affairs and conventional mortgages from primary lenders and sells them to investors. The index measures mortgage commitments for delivery within 30 to 60 days that is the required net yield on mortgage loans that lenders sell to FNMA, which in turn sells them to investors.

Forbearance: Refrain from doing something (i.e., collecting a debt).

Foreclosure: Legal process that leads to the repossession and sale of real property that was pledged as collateral on a mortgage debt.

Foreign currency surcharge: A new charge imposed by some credit card issuers that imposes a fee on purchases made in a foreign currency.

Foreign Spending: When you make a purchase in a foreign currency. The charge will automatically be converted to your country's currency by the rate of exchange on that day.

Fraud Alert: A notation on a consumer's credit report that tells creditors and other third parties that the consumer may have been a victim of fraud or identity theft. It asks the credit issuer to take additional verification steps before granting credit, such as contacting the consumer at a specified phone number. Policies regarding fraud alerts vary by credit issuer, and can include calling the consumer, asking the applicant for additional proofs of identity or simply denying the application. Any consumer may raise a fraud alert for free by contacting Experian, Equifax or TransUnion. The credit reporting agency contacted should forward the fraud alert to the other two. Initial fraud alerts expire after 90 days, but can be renewed. Seven-year fraud alerts require a copy of a valid identity theft report filed with law enforcement. Those on active duty may request an active duty alert, which expires after one year.

Fraud Protection: Protects your credit card in case it is lost or stolen. You will not have to pay for any unauthorized purchases. Please read your credit card agreement to find the exact conditions of your protection.

Fraudulent Transfers (Conveyances): Transfer of property or an obligation made within one year before the filing date of the bankruptcy petition that was made with the intent to hinder, delay or defraud creditors.

Freeloader: A credit card industry term for a card holder who pays off the balance monthly and therefore pays no interest or fees.

Fresh Start: The characterization of a debtor's status after bankruptcy, i.e., free of most debts. (Giving debtors, a fresh start is one purpose of the Bankruptcy Code).

FSUC: Federal Savings and Loan Insurance Corp. A federal institution that insures deposits of federally chartered savings and loan associations.

Future Purchase Option: Life and health insurance provisions that guarantee the insured the right to buy additional coverage without proving insurability. Also known as "guaranteed insurability option."

General Account: All premiums are paid into an insurer's general account. Thus, buyers are subject to credit-risk exposure to the insurance company, which is low but not zero.

General Liability Insurance: Insurance designed to protect business owners and operators from a wide variety of liability exposures. Exposures could include liability arising from accidents resulting from the insured's premises or operations, products sold by the insured, operations completed by the insured, and contractual liability.

Gift Card: A pre-paid debit card purchases as a gift. Retailers issue gift cards to be used only in their stores. Major credit cards also issue gift cards, which can be used wherever those cards are accepted.

Good Faith: With good intentions (i.e., with most accurate information available.

Good Standing: Condition of a credit account that is currently paid as agreed.

Governmental Instrumentality: An agency of the government.

126

Grace Period: If the credit card user does not carry a balance; the grace period is the interest free time a lender allows between the transaction date and the billing date. The standard grace period is usually between 20 and 30 days. If there is no grace period, finance charges will accrue the moment a purchase is made with the credit card. People who carry a balance on their credit cards have no grace period.

Gross Income: This is all the money, goods and property you receive during the year before you reduce it by using adjustments, deductions or exemptions. People who use the barter system have to include the value of whatever they have received in exchange for services as part of their gross income.

Gross Leverage: The sum of net leverage and ceded reinsurance leverage. This ratio measures a company's gross exposure to pricing errors in its current book of business, to errors of estimating its liabilities, and exposure to its reinsurers.

Guaranteed Insurability Option: See "future purchase option."

Guaranteed Issue Right: The right to purchase insurance without physical examination; the present and past physical condition of the applicant are not considered.

Guaranteed Renewable: A policy provision in many products which guarantees the policy owner the right to renew coverage at every policy anniversary date. The company does not have the right to cancel coverage except for nonpayment of premiums by the policy owner; however, the company can raise rates if they choose.

Guarantor: One who guarantors the debt or obligation of another.

Guaranty: A pledge or promise given as security for payment of a debt or obligation.

Guaranty Association: An organization of life insurance companies within a state responsible for covering the financial obligations of a member company that becomes insolvent.

Hacker: Someone with expertise in computer systems and knows how to enter them in an unauthorized fashion. Hackers may be simply curious or malicious in intent.

Hard Inquiry: An item on a person's credit report that indicates that someone has asked for a copy of the individual's report. Hard inquiries are requests that result from a person applying for credit, such as a mortgage, a car loan, a credit card or a rental application. They are included in the formula for determining a person's credit score.

Hazard: A circumstance that increases the likelihood or probable severity of a loss. For example, the storing of explosives in a home basement is a hazard that increases the probability of an explosion.

Hazardous Activity: Bungee jumping, scuba diving, horse riding and other activities not generally covered by standard insurance policies. For insurers that do provide cover for such activities, it is unlikely they will cover liability and personal accident, which should be provided by the company hosting the activity.

Health Maintenance Organization (HMO): Prepaid group health insurance plan that entitles members to services of participating physicians, hospitals and clinics. Emphasis is on preventative medicine, and members must use contracted health-care providers.

Health Reimbursement Arrangement: Owners of high-deductible health plans who are not qualified for a health savings account can use an HRA.

Health Savings Account: Plan that allows you to contribute pre-tax money to be used for qualified medical expenses. HSAs, which are portable, must be linked to a high-deductible health insurance policy.

Household Income: The total income of all members of a household. An important yardstick used by lenders evaluating applications for joint credit.

Hurricane Deductible: Amount you must pay out-of-pocket before hurricane insurance will kick in. Many insurers in hurricane-prone states are selling homeowners insurance policies with percentage deductibles for storm damage, instead of the traditional dollar deductibles used for claims such as fire and theft. Percentage deductibles vary from one percent of a home's insured value to 15 percent, depending on many factors that differ by state and insurer.

Impaired Insurer: An insurer which is in financial difficulty to the point where its ability to meet financial obligations regulatory requirements is in question.

Indemnification: Act of agreeing to compensate someone for any loss or damage.

Indemnity: Restoration to the victim of a loss by payment, repair or replacement.

Independent Bank: A bank that is locally owned and operated, and not associated with a bank holding company. Also referred to as a community bank.

Independent Insurance Agents & Brokers of America (IIABA): formerly the Independent Insurance Agents of America (IIAA), this is a member organization of independent agents and brokers monitoring and affecting industry issues. Numerous state associations are affiliated with the IIABA.

Identity Theft: The act of stealing an individual's personal information to steal their credit cards, bank account, and other finances. An identity thief will take your social security number, birth date, address, name, and bank account information.

Income Taxes: Incurred income taxes (including income taxes on capital gains) reported in each annual statement for that year.

Index: A table of yields or interest rates being paid on debt (such as Treasury notes or bank deposits) that is used to determine interest rate changes for adjustable rate mortgages and other variable rate loans such as credit card debt. Some of the most common indices are: the one-year Treasury Constant Maturity Yield, The Federal Home Loan Bank (FHLB) 11TH District Cost of Funds, prime rate as listed in the Wall Street Journal.

Indexed Rate: The sum of the published index plus the margin. For example, if the index is 9 percent and the margin 2.75 percent, the indexed rate is 11.75 percent.

Inflation Protection: An optional property coverage endorsement offered by some insurers that increases the policy's limits of insurance during the policy term to keep pace with inflation.

Installment Contract: A purchase agreement in which the buyer makes a series of payments.

Insurable Interest: Interest in property such that loss or destruction of the property could cause a financial loss.

Insurance Adjuster: A representative of the insurer who seeks to determine the extent of the insurer's liability for loss when a claim is submitted. Independent insurance adjusters are hired by insurance companies on an "as needed" basis and might work for several insurance companies at the same time. Independent adjusters charge insurance companies both by the hour and by miles traveled. Public adjusters work for the insured in the settlement of claims and receive a percentage of the claim as their fee. A.M. Best's Directory of Recommended Insurance Attorneys and Adjusters lists independent adjusters only.

Insurance Attorneys: An attorney who practices the law as it relates to insurance matters. Attorneys might be solo practitioners or work as part of a law firm. Insurance companies who retain attorneys to defend them against law suits might hire staff attorneys to work for them in-house or they might retain attorneys on an as-needed basis. A.M. Best's Directory of Recommended Attorneys and Adjusters lists insurance defense attorneys who concentrate their practice in insurance defense such as coverage issues, bad faith, malpractice, products liability, and workers' compensation.

Insurance Institute of America (IIA): An organization which develops programs and conducts national examinations in general insurance, risk management, management, adjusting, underwriting, auditing and loss control management.

Insurance Regulatory Information System (IRIS): Introduced by the National Association of Insurance Commissioners in 1974 to identify insurance companies that might require further regulatory review.

Interchange Fee: The fee paid by retailers to banks and card issuers for every transaction they process. A PIN based transaction costs less than a signature based transaction.

Interest: Money paid for a borrower's use of money, calculated as a percentage of the money borrowed and paid over a specified time. 2. A right to, or share title to property.

Interest Accrual Rate: Percentage a borrower pays for the use of money, usually expressed as an annual percentage.

Interest Crediting Methods: There are at least 35 interest-crediting methods that insurers use. They usually involve some combination of point-to-point, annual reset, yield spread, averaging, or high-water mark.

Interest Rate: The amount charged per year on a personal or home loan. The rate varies according to the type of loan. Or, the percentage of interest paid for money in deposit accounts, without regard to compounding, shown as an annual figure.

Interest Rate Cap: A limit on how much a borrower's percentage rate can increase of decrease at rate adjustment periods and over the life of the loan.

Interest Rate Ceiling: Specified in the loan agreement, the highest percentage a lender can charge for an adjustable rate mortgage.

Internet Bank: A bank that exists only on the Internet without and "brick and mortar" branches. By eliminating the overhead costs of structures, Internet banks consistently offer interest rates, including money market yields that are higher than the national average. Also known as a virtual bank.

Interstate Banking: Bank expansion across state lines through the use of bank holding companies and acquisitions of existing banks.

Introductory (or Intro) Rate: The low rate charged by a lender for an initial period to entice borrowers to accept the credit terms. After the introductory period is over, the rate charged increases to the indexed rate or the stated interest rate. Often called a teaser rate.

Investment Income: The return received by insurers from their investment portfolios including interest, dividends and realized capital gains on stocks. It doesn't include the value of any stocks or bonds that the company currently owns.

Investments in Affiliates: Bonds, stocks, collateral loans, short-term investments in affiliated and real estate properties occupied by the company.

Issuer: A financial institution that provides a credit card.

Issuing Financial Institution: The financial institution that issues a credit card and bills the customer for purchases made against the card account.

Joint Credit: Issued to a couple based on both of their assets, incomes and credit reports. It generally results in a higher credit limit, but makes both parties responsible for repaying the debt.

Joint Liability: The responsibility of two or more people to repay a debt.

Joint Petition: One bankruptcy petition filed by a husband and wife together.

Judgment: A court decision.

Judgment Proof: Immune from results of a judgment (i.e., having no assets from which a creditor can collect a money judgment).

Junior Interest: An interest (typically in property that is inferior to another's interest).

Key: A password needed to decipher encrypted data.

Laddering: Purchasing bond investments that mature at different time intervals.

Lapse Ratio: The ratio of the number of life insurance policies that lapsed within a given period to the number in force at the beginning of that period.

Late Charge: A fee imposed on a borrower for not paying on time.

Late Fee: A charge received from missing the payment due date. If a person is mailing a payment they should mail it at least 5 days before the due date.

Late Payment: A sum a borrower sends to a lender that is received past the date when it was due.

Late Payment Fee: Charge imposed on a debtor for not paying on time.

Least Expensive Alternative Treatment: The amount an insurance company will pay based on its determination of cost for a particular procedure.

Lender: A person or entity that loans money to another.

Leverage or Capitalization: Measures the exposure of a company's surplus to various operating and financial practices. A highly leveraged, or poorly capitalized, company can show a high return on surplus, but might be exposed to a high risk of instability.

Liabilities: A borrower's debts and legal obligations.

Liability: Broadly, any legally enforceable obligation. The term is most commonly used in a pecuniary sense.

Liability Insurance: Insurance that pays and renders service on behalf of an insured for loss arising out of his responsibility, due to negligence, to others imposed by law or assumed by contract.

LIBOR Rate: LIBOR stands for London Interbank Offered Rate. It's the rate of interest at which banks offer to lend money to one another in the wholesale money markets in London. It is a standard financial index used in U.S. capital markets and can be found in the Wall Street Journal. In general, its changes have been smaller than changes in the prime rate. It's an index that is used to set the cost of various variable rate loans, including credit cards and adjustable rate mortgages.

Licensed: Indicates the company is incorporated (or chartered) in another state but is a licensed (admitted) insurer for this state to write specific lines of business for which it qualifies.

Licensed for Reinsurance Only: Indicates the company is a licensed (admitted) insurer to write reinsurance on risks in this state.

Lien: Interest in a piece of property that guarantees a debt.

Life Cap: A limit on how much a borrower's percentage rate can increase or decrease over the term of the loan.

Life of the Balance: An interest rate that is applied to a balance until it is paid off. The interest rate will not change.

Lifetime Reserve Days: Sixty additional days Medicare pays for when you are hospitalized for more than 90 days in a benefit period. These days can only be used once during your lifetime. For each lifetime reserve day, Medicare pays all covered costs except for a daily coinsurance amount.

Line of Credit: The amount of credit extended from a lender to a borrower. In the case of a credit card, it is the maximum you can charge to your card.

Liquidation: A sale of a debtor's property, with the proceeds to be used for the benefit of creditors.

Liquidity: The ability to convert assets to cash quickly, without significant losses.

Living Benefits: This feature allows you, under certain circumstances, to receive the proceeds of your life insurance policy before you die. Such circumstances include terminal or catastrophic illness, the need for long-term care, or confinement to a nursing home. Also known as "accelerated death benefits."

Lloyd's: Generally refers to Lloyd's of London, England, an institution within which individual underwriters accept or reject the risks offered to them. The Lloyd's Corp. provides the support facility for their activities.

Lloyds Organizations: These organizations are voluntary unincorporated associations of individuals. Each individual assumes a specified portion of the liability under each policy issued. The underwriters operate through a common attorney-in-fact appointed for this purpose by the underwriters. The laws of most states contain some provisions

Loan: Exchange of funds with a promise to repay under certain terms, including time period, interest rate, and frequency of payments.

Loan application: A document in which a prospective borrower details his or her financial situation to qualify for a loan.

Loan application fee: A sum charged by a lender for accepting a document in which a prospective borrower details his or her financial situation to qualify for a loan.

Loan -to-value ratio (LTV): The percentage of the home's price that is paid for by a mortgage. On a $100,000 house, if the buyer makes a $20,000 down payment and borrows $80,000, the mortgage is 80 percent of the price of the house. Therefore, the loan-to-value ratio is computed using the appraised value of the home, not the sale price.

Log In: The procedure by which a customer "enters" an online financial institution. When logging in, customers enter their passwords to gain access to a secure area of the institution's website, where they can view their financial records and take action, such as online bill payment.

Loss Adjustment Expenses: Expenses incurred to investigate and settle losses.

Loss and Loss-Adjustment Reserves to Policy Holder Surplus Ratio: The higher the multiple of loss reserves to surplus, the more a company's solvency is dependent upon having and maintaining reserve adequacy.

Losses and Loss-Adjustment Expenses: This represents the total reserves for unpaid losses and loss-adjustment expenses, including reserves for any incurred but not reported losses, and supplemental reserves established by the company. It is the total for all lines of business and all accident years.

Loss Control: All methods taken to reduce the frequency and/or severity of losses including exposure avoidance, loss prevention, loss reduction, segregation of exposure units and non-insurance transfer risk. A combination of risk control techniques with risk financing techniques forms the nucleus of a risk management program. The use of appropriate insurance, avoidance of risk, loss control, risk retention, self-insuring, and other techniques that minimize the risks of a business, individual, or organization.

Loss Ratio: The ratio of incurred losses and loss-adjustment expenses to net premiums earned. This ratio measures the company's underlying profitability, or loss experience, on its total book of business.

Loss Reserve: The estimated liability, as it would appear in an insurer's financial statement, for unpaid insurance claims or losses that have occurred as of a given evaluation date. Usually includes losses incurred, but not reported (IBNR), losses due but not yet paid, and amounts not yet due. For individual claims, the loss reserve is the estimate of what will ultimately be paid out on that claim.

Losses Incurred (Pure Losses): Net paid losses during the current year plus the change in loss reserves since the prior year end.

Major Bank: Banks that provides services to the agent banks in a chain.

Margin: Expressed as percentage points, the amount that a lender adds to an index to arrive at the final interest rate. For example, if the index is 9 percent and the margin 2.75 percent, the final interest rate is 11.75 percent.

Mastercard: A product of Mastercard International, is distributed by issuing financial institutions around the world. Card holders borrow money against a credit line and pay it back with interest, if the balance is carried over from month to month.

Medical Loss Ratio: Total health benefits divided by total premium.

Member Bank: A commercial bank with membership in the Federal Reserve System, and which maintains reserve deposits in the Federal Reserve Bank in its district.

Member Month: Total number of health plan participants who are members for each month.

Merged Credit Report: A combined summary of one's credit history from the three largest credit bureaus: Equifax, Experian and TransUnion.

Minimum Finance Charge: The interest applied to your balance is under $.50 you will be charged $.50 in interest. If you do not pay your balance in full, but only have a small balance remaining you will probably receive a minimum finance charge. Many credit cards have one.

Minimum Payment: The least amount a person must pay a credit card company for their statement. Some card issuers will set a high minimum, if they are uncertain of the cardholder's ability to pay. Most card issuers require a minimum payment of 2 percent of the outstanding balance.

Modification: A change in terms of the loan agreement.

Monthly Periodic Rate: The interest rate factor used to calculate the interest charges on a monthly basis. The factor equals the yearly rate divided by 12. See periodic rate.

Monthly Treasury Average (1 year): An index determined by the monthly average of one-year Treasury bills. Commonly used as a benchmark for adjustable rate mortgages.

MOP: (Manner of Payment). Might head the column on a credit report that lists the payment history.

Mortality and Expense Risk Fees: A charge that covers such annuity contract guarantees as such death benefits.

Mortgage: The pledge of property as security for a loan, usually real property.

Mortgage Insurance Policy: In life and health insurance, a policy covering a mortgagor with benefits intended to pay off the balance due on a mortgage upon the insured's death, or to meet the payments due on a mortgage in case of the insured's death or disability.

Mutual Insurance Companies: Companies with no capital stock, and owned by policyholders. The earnings of the company-over and above the payments of the losses, operating expenses and reserves, are the property of the policyholders. There are two types of mutual insurance companies. Nonassessable mutual charges a fixed premium and the policyholders cannot be assessed further. Legal reserves and surplus are maintained to provide payment of all claims. Assessable mutual are companies that charge an initial fixed premium and, if that isn't sufficient, might assess policyholders to meet losses in excess of the premiums that have been charged.

Named Perils: Perils specifically covered on insured property.

National Association of Insurance Commissioners (NAIC): Association of state insurance commissioners whose purpose is to promote uniformity of insurance regulation, monitor insurance solvency and develop model laws for passage by state legislatures.

National Bank: A bank chartered by the federal government and a mandatory member of the Federal Reserve System.

National Credit Union Association: Created in 1970 to charter and supervise federal credit unions.

National Credit Union Share Insurance Fund: Insurers credit union deposits.

National Foundation for Consumer Credit: A nonprofit organization that educates consumers about using credit wisely. The NFCC is the parent group for Consumer Credit Counseling Service.

National Issuers: The overwhelming majority of credit cards in the United States come from a handful of national issuers, such as First USA, MBNA America and Bank of America. They often originate from lender friendly states such as Delaware and South Dakota that impose no limits on what cardholders can be charged.

NCUA: National Credit Union Association: Created in 1970 to charter and supervise federal credit unions.

NCUSIF: National Credit Union Share Insurance Fund: Insures credit union deposits.

Negligence: To omit doing something through indifference or carelessness.

Net Income: The total after-tax earnings generated from operations and realized capital gains as reported in the company's NAIC annual statement on page 4, line 16.

Net Investment Income: This item represents investment income earned during the year less investment expenses and depreciation on real estate. Investment expenses are the expenses related to generating investment income and capital gains, but exclude income taxes.

Net Leverage: The sum of a company's net premium written to policyholder surplus and net liabilities to policyholder surplus. This ratio measures the combination of a company's net exposure to pricing errors in its current book of business and errors of estimation in its net liabilities after reinsurance, in relation to policyholder surplus.

Net Liabilities to Policyholder Surplus: Net liabilities expressed as a ratio to policyholder surplus. Net liabilities equal total liabilities less conditional reserves, plus encumbrances on real estate, less the smaller of receivables from or payable to affiliates. This ratio measures company's exposures to errors of estimation in its loss reserves and all other liabilities. Loss-reserve leverage is generally the key component of net liability leverage. The higher the loss-reserve leverage the more critical a company's solvency depends upon maintaining reserve adequacy.

Net Premium: The amount of premium minus the agent's commission. Also, the premium necessary to cover only anticipated losses, before loading to cover other expenses.

Net Premiums Earned: The adjustment of net premiums written for the increase or decrease of the company's liability for unearned premiums during the year. Ehen an insurance company's business increase from year to year, the earned premiums will usually be less than the written premiums. With the increased volume, the premiums are considered fully paid at the inception of the policy so that, at the end of a calendar period, the company must set up premiums representing the unexpired terms of the policies. On a decreasing volume, the reverse is true.

Net Premiums Written: Represents gross premium written, direct and reinsurance assumed, less reinsurance ceded.

Net Premiums Written to Policyholder Surplus (IRIS): This ratio measures a company's net retained premiums written after reinsurance assumed and ceded, in relation to its surplus. This ratio measures the company's exposure to pricing errors in its current book of business.

Net Underwriting Income: Net Premiums earned less incurred losses, loss-adjustment expenses, underwriting expenses incurred, and dividends to policyholders.

Net Worth: The total value of all assets, such as house, car, furniture and investments, minus all debts, such as mortgages and credit card bills.

Neutral: Account that is not rated on a credit report due to newness or some other reason. It is neither positive nor negative on the report.

NFCC: The National Foundation for Consumer Credit is a nonprofit organization that educates consumers about using credit wisely. The NFCC is the parent group for Consumer Credit Counseling Service.

Niche Bank: Smaller banks that cater to particular communities or certain industries. These banks have been thriving in the fallout from mega-bank mergers.

Noncancelable: Contract terms, including costs that can never be changed.

Nondischargeable Debt: A debt that cannot be eliminated in bankruptcy. Examples include some taxes and, usually, federally guaranteed education loans.

Non-Recourse Mortgage: A home loan in which the borrower can never owe more than the home's value at the time the loan is repaid.

Nonstandard Auto (High Risk Auto or Substandard Auto): Insurance for motorists who have poor driving records or have been canceled or refused insurance. The premium is much higher than standard auto due to the additional risks.

Nonverification: Lapse of the 30 days that a credit bureau is given under law to verify a debt at the consumer's request.

NSF: Also referred to as a returned or "bounced" check charge or non-sufficient funds fee. The amount of money charged to an account holder whose account has insufficient funds available to pay the check, which is returned to the party who cashed it unpaid. (The bank did not advance the funds to cover the check.)

Obligor: One who is obligated to act (i.e., one who owes money).

Occurrence: An event that results in an insured loss. In some lines of business, such as liability, an occurrence is distinguished from accident in that the loss doesn't have to be sudden and fortuitous and can result from continuous or repeated exposure which results in bodily injury or property damage neither expected not intended by the insured.

Office of Comptroller of the Currency: Known as OCC: Charters, regulates and supervises all national banks. It also supervises all federal branches and agencies of foreign banks.

Office of Thrift Supervision: A bureau of the U.S. Treasury Department established in August 1989. OTS has the authority to charter federal Thrift Institutions and serves as the primary regulator of approximately 2,000 federal and state chartered thrifts.

Offline Debit Card: Cards that share traits of both ATM and credit cards. Offline debit cards have the VISA or Mastercard logo on them and can be issued by a bank, either instead of or in addition to an ATM card. These cards can be used at any establishment that displays the VISA or MasterCard logo, but using them doesn't access a line of credit, it debits a customer's checking account. It is "offline" because the account isn't directly accessed, there's a delay of 24 to 72 hours before the debit is made in the account. If you sign a slip of paper to conclude the transaction, it was offline. In the U.S., no Personal Identification Number (PIN) is required to use an offline debit card.

One-Year Treasury Constant Maturity: An index published by the Federal Reserve Board based on the average yield of a range of Treasury securities, all adjusted to the equivalent of a one-year maturity. Yields on Treasury securities at constant maturity are determined by the U.S. Treasury from the daily yield curve. That is based on the closing market-bid yields on actively traded Treasury securities in the over the counter market.

Online Banking: Access by personal computer or terminal to bank information, accounts and certain transactions via the financial institution's web site on the Internet. Also known as Internet banking.

Online Bill Payment: A service offered by online banks, usually for a small monthly fee, that relieves consumers from having to write checks and lick stamps to pay their monthly bills. Online bill payment systems allow people to enter the names of their creditors and the numbers of their utility accounts and pay virtually all routine bills.

Online Debit Card: An online debit card that deducts funds from the bank account immediately, as soon as the card is used. It may have the VISA or MasterCard logo, or only the issuing bank's logo, like an ATM card. There is no delay for processing the transaction. The money is immediately deducted from your account. In the U.S., if you entered a Personal Identification Number (PIN) during the transaction, it was online.

Online Statement: A credit card statement that can be viewed over the internet. Please refer to statement for more information.

Open-End Credit: A line of credit that may be used up to a set limit. Also called a charge account or revolving credit.

Operating Cash Flow: Measures the funds generated from insurance operations, which includes the change in cash and invested assets attributed to underwriting activities, net investment income and federal income taxes. This measure excludes stockholder dividends, capital contributions, unrealized capital gains/losses and various noninsurance related transactions with affiliates. This test measures a company's ability to meet current obligations through the internal generation of funds from insurance operations. Negative balances might indicate unprofitable underwriting results or low yielding assets.

Operating Ratio (IRIS): Combined ratio less the net investment income ratio (net investment income to net premiums earned). The operating ratio measures a company's overall operational profitability from underwriting and investment activities. This ratio doesn't reflect other operating income/expenses, capital gains or income taxes. An operating ratio of more than 100 indicates a company is unable to generate profits from its underwriting and investment activities.

Oral Agreement: A spoken, unwritten legal agreement that is as valid as a written agreement, in most cases, though its existence is more difficult to prove. Oral agreements are not enforceable in real estate.

Original Principal Balance: The amount borrowed.

Other Income/Expenses: This item represents miscellaneous sources of operating income or expenses that principally relate to premium finance income or changes for uncollectible premium and reinsurance business.

OTS: Short for Office of Thrift Supervision. A bureau of the U.S. Treasury Department established in August 1989. OTS has the authority to charter federal Thrift Institutions and serves as the primary regulator of approximately 2,000 federal and state chartered thrifts.

Out-of-Pocket Limit: A predetermined amount of money that an individual must pay before insurance will pay 100% for an individual's health care expenses.

Outstanding Balance: The amount of money a customer owes to a bank. This includes the principal and interest.

Overall Liquidity Ratio: Total admitted assets divided by total liabilities less conditional reserves. This ratio indicates a company's ability to cover net liabilities with total assets. This ratio doesn't address the quality and marketability of premium balances, affiliated investments and other un-invested assets.

Over the Limit Fee: A charge for exceeding the limit of a credit card.

Overdraft: The amount that a check exceeds the available balance in the payer's account, also insufficient funds.

Overdraft Protection: A service that allows a checking account to be linked to another savings or line of credit to provide protection against insufficient funds or overdrafts.

Own Occupation: Insurance contract provision that allows policyholders to collect benefits if they can no longer work in their own occupation.

Paid-Up Additional Insurance: An option that allows the policyholder to use policy dividends and/or additional premiums to buy additional insurance on the same plan as the basic policy and at a face amount determined by the insured's attained age.

Participation Rate: In equity-indexed annuities, a participation rate determines how much of the gain in the index will be credited to the annuity. For example, the insurance company may set the participation rate at 80%, which means the annuity would only be credited with 80% of the gain experienced by the index.

Payment Cap: A contractual limit on the size of the monthly payment of an adjustable rate mortgage or other variable rate loan.

Payment History: Summary of the payments made on a specific loan obligation, usually stated as how many payments were made on time, 30 days late, 60 days late, or 90 days late.

PC Banking: A service that allows a bank customer to obtain account information and perform certain bank transactions through a personal computer.

Penalty Rate: Several percentage points higher than a card's current annual percentage rate, which goes into effect after two late payments. On some cards, a single late payment triggers a penalty rate.

Peril: The cause of a possible loss.

Periodic Rate: The interest rate for a specific amount of time usually either monthly or daily. It is determined by dividing the Annual Percentage

Rate by the amount of time. For months' time=12 and for days' time=365.

Personal Finance Manager: Specialized computer programs that help customers carry out a variety of personal finance activities. These programs typically allow consumers to do much of their work off-line, and then dial in to complete their bank transaction.

Personal Identification Number (PIN): A number code used like a password, usually consisting of four to six digits. You use this number to get cash from ATMS, and when you are talking to a customer service representative they may ask for your PIN for verification.

Personal Injury Protection: Pays basic expenses for an insured and his or her family in states with no-fault auto insurance. No-fault laws generally require drivers to carry both liability insurance and personal injury protection coverage to pay for basic needs of the insured, such as medical expenses, in the event of an accident.

Personal Lines: Insurance for individuals and families, such as private: passenger auto and homeowner's insurance.

Personal Property: Any property that is moveable as opposed to real estate or fixed to real estate. Also, referred to as chattel.

PIN: Personal Identification Number. A confidential personal identification code, usually consisting of four to six digits, used by bank customers to access their account balances when using a self-service automated teller machine (ATM).

Point-of-Sale: An electronic payment system for retail goods and services, through the use of credit cards or debit cards that directly access and deduct funds from a customer's checking account. Also known as POS.

Point-of-Service Plan: Health insurance policy that allows the employee to choose between in-network and out-of-network care each time medical treatment is needed.

POS: Point of Sale. An electronic payment system for retail goods and services, through the use of credit cards or debit cards that directly access and deduct funds from a customer's checking account.

Policy: The written contract effecting insurance, or the certificate thereof, by whatever name called, and including all clause, riders, endorsements, and papers attached thereto and made a part thereof.

Policyholder Dividend Ratio: The ratio of dividends to policyholders related to net premiums earned.

Policyholder Surplus: The sum of paid in capital, paid in and contributed surplus, and net earned surplus, including voluntary contingency reserves. It also is the difference between total admitted assets and total liabilities.

Policy or Sales Illustration: Material used by an agent and insured to show how a policy may perform under a variety of conditions and over a number of years.

Power of Attorney: A document in which the signer authorizes someone to conduct business in his or her name. Signing title documents and checks, for example.

Pre-Approved: A person has only passed a preliminary screening. It does not mean a person is guaranteed a credit card. A credit card company can spurn the customers it invited with "pre-approved" junk mail if it doesn't like the applicants credit rating.

Pre-Existing Condition: A coverage limitation included in many health policies which states that certain physical or mental conditions, either previously diagnosed or which would normally be expected to require treatment prior to issue, will not be covered under the new policy for a specified period of time.

Preferred Auto: Auto coverage for drivers who have never had an accident and operates vehicles according to law, Drivers are not a risk for any insurance company that writes auto insurance, and no insurance company would be afraid to take them on as risk.

Preferred Provider Organization: Network of medical providers who charge on a fee-for-service basis, but are paid on a negotiated, discounted fee schedule.

Premium: The price of insurance protection for a specified risk for a specified period of time.

Premium Balances: Premiums and agents' balances in course of collection; premiums, agents' balances and installments booked but deferred and not yet due; bills receivable, taken for premiums and accrued retrospective premiums.

Premium Earned: The amount of the premium that has been paid for in advance that has been "earned" by virtue of the fact that time has passed without claim. A three-year policy that has been paid in advance and is one year old would have only partly earned the premium.

Premium to Surplus Ratio: This ratio is designed to measure the ability of the insurer to absorb above-average losses and the insurer's financial strength. The ratio is computed by dividing net premiums written by surplus. An insurance company's surplus is the amount by which assets exceed liabilities. The ratio is computed by dividing net premiums written by surplus. For example, a company with $2 in net premiums written for every $1 of surplus has a 2-to-1 premium to surplus ratio. The lower the ratio, the greater the company's financial strength. State regulators have established a premium-to-surplus ratio of no higher than 3-to-1 as a guideline.

Premium Unearned: That part of the premium applicable to the unexpired part of the policy period.

Prepayment Penalty: A lender's charge to the borrower for paying off the loan before the end of the term. It is present in some mortgages, preventing borrowers from rapid refinancing.

Pretax Operating Income: Pretax operating earnings before any capital gains generated from underwriting, investment and other miscellaneous operating sources.

Pretax Return on Revenue: A measure of a company's operating profitability and is calculated by dividing pretax operating earnings by net premiums earned.

Previous Balance: A way credit card companies determine how much interest is owed. It is the previous balance multiplied by the interest rate.

Previous Balance Method: Same meaning as previous balance.

Primary User: Debtor signed on an account that is primarily responsible for repaying the debt.

Prime for Life: A type of line of credit loan coveted by consumers that fixes the interest at the prime rate for the life of the loan.

Prime Rate: A common benchmark for consumer and business loans set by banks, usually at a level 3 percentage points higher than the Fed Funds rate. The rate given to consumers on their loans is often determined as the prime rate plus a certain percentage, which represents the lender's assessment of the risk in lending, plus its profit margin.

Principal: 1. The amount of money borrowed. 2. The amount of money owed, excluding interest. 3. The client of a real estate agent.

Private Label Cards: A private label card is issued by a retail outlet, such as a department store or gasoline company, and contain the logo of the retailer. It is accepted only by the retailer who issued it. Retailers partner with a bank or a card issuing Management Company to back the cards.

Private-Passenger Auto Insurance Policyholder Risk Profile: This refers to the risk profile of auto insurance policyholders and can be divided into three categories: standard, nonstandard and preferred. In the eyes of an insurance company, it is the type of business (or the quality of driver) that the company has chosen to take on.

Profit: A measure of the competence and ability of management to provide viable insurance products at competitive prices and maintain a financially strong company for both policyholders and stockholders.

Pro Rata: In proportion to something, according to a certain rate.

Protected Cell Company (PCC): A PCC is a single legal entity that operates segregated accounts, or cells, each of which is legally protected from the liabilities of the company's other accounts. An individual client's account is insulated from the gains and losses of other accounts, such that the PCC sponsor and each client is protected against liquidation activities by creditors in the event of insolvency of another client.

Public Record: Records that are kept by a governmental body and available to the public for review.

Punitive Damages: Compensation awarded for an injury or wrong that is intended to punish the one who committed such injury or wrong.

Punitive Rate: In credit card terms, the punitive rate is the highest interest rates the company charges. It can be imposed when consumers violate their contract agreements by acts such as paying late or exceeding their credit limits.

Purchase Money Mortgage: Mortgage given by the buyer back to the seller of property.

Qualified High-Deductible Health Plan-A health plan with lower premiums that covers health-care expenses only after the insured has paid each year a large amount out of pocket or from another source. To qualify as a health plan coupled with a Health Savings Account, the Internal Revenue Code requires the deductible to be at least $1,000 for an individual and $2,000 for a family. High-deductible plans are also known as catastrophic plans.

Qualified Versus Non-Qualified Policies: Qualified plans are those employee benefit plans that meet Internal Revenue Service requirements as stated in IRS Code Section 401a. When a plan is approved, contributions made by the employer are tax deductible expenses.

Qualifying Event: An occurrence that triggers an insured's protection.

Qualifying Ratios: As calculated by lenders, the percentage of income that is spent on housing debt and combined household debt. The first qualifying ratio, called the front ratio, is the percentage of monthly before tax income that goes toward a house payment. The back ratio is the sum of the house payment and all other monthly debt such as credit cards, car payments and student loans divided by before tax income.

Quick Assets: Assets that are quickly convertible into cash.

Quick Liquidity Ratio: Quick assets divided by net liabilities plus ceded reinsurance balances payable. Quick assets are defined as the sum of cash, unaffiliated short-term investments, unaffiliated bonds maturing within one year, government bonds maturing within five years, and 80% of unaffiliated common stocks. These assets can be quickly converted into cash in the case of an emergency.

Quitclaim Deed: Transfer of title to real estate that does not contain any guaranties or warranties.

Rate: Percentage a borrower pays for the use of money, usually expressed as an annual percentage.

Rate Index: A table of yields or interest rates being paid on debts (such as Treasury notes or bank deposits) that is used to determine interest rate changes for adjustable rate mortgages and other variable rate loans.

Reaffirmation agreement: An agreement by a Chapter 7 debtor to continue paying a dischargeable debt after the bankruptcy, usually to keep collateral or mortgage property that would otherwise be subject to repossession.

Real Property: Real estate; land.

Reasonable Time: Amount of time that a credit bureau has to respond to a consumer dispute usually up to eight weeks.

Rebate Card: This is a credit card that allows the customer to accumulate cash, merchandise or services based on card usage.

Receiver: An appointed or authorized official who oversees the property of the debtor. This official will either manage the property for the purpose of enforcing a lien against it or for the general distribution of the item(s) to the debtor's creditors.

Recent Activity: Purchases a person makes after the billing cycle is over. These purchases will be included in your net billing cycle.

Recession: A prolonged period (popularly defined as two successive quarters) in which economic activity shrinks.

Reciprocal Insurance Exchange: Unincorporated groups of individuals, firms or corporations, commonly termed subscribers, who mutually insure one another, each separately assuming his or her share of each risk. Its chief administrator is an attorney-in-fact.

Recurring Debt: Debt that occurs periodically, including such obligations as credit card payments, child support, car loans, and others that will not be paid off within a relatively short period of time (6-10 months).

Redemption: Debtors may keep exempt secured property even though they owe money on it by paying the creditor the collateral value of the property rather than the amount of the debt. Note that in some cases the "value" of the collateral may be less than the amount owed on it. In these cases, it may be advantageous for the debtor to redeem the property.

Re-Entry: The allowance for level-premium term policy owners to qualify for another level-premium period, generally with new evidence of insurability.

Regional Bank: A bank with a primary market in a regional or metropolitan area but takes deposits from throughout the state in which it is located. It is typically more expansive than a community bank, but more restrictive than a national financial institution.

Regulation Z: A rule, enforcing by the Federal Reserve Board and implementing the Truth-in-Lending Act that requires lenders to disclose all credit related costs including the annual percentage rate.

Reinsurance: In effect, insurance that an insurance company buys for its own protection. The risk of loss is spread so a disproportionately large loss under a single policy doesn't fall on one company. Reinsurance enables an insurance company to expand its capacity; stabilize its underwriting results; finance its expanding volume; secure catastrophe protection against shock losses; withdraw from a line of business or a geographical area within a specified time period.

Reinsurance Ceded: The unit of insurance transferred to a reinsurer by a ceding company.

Reinsurance Recoverable to Policyholder Surplus: Measures a company's dependence upon its reinsurers and the potential exposure to adjustments on such reinsurance. It's determined from the total ceded reinsurance recoverable due from non-U.S. affiliates for paid losses, unpaid losses, losses incurred but not reported (IBNR), unearned premiums and commissions less funds held from reinsurers expressed as a percent of policyholder surplus.

Remaining Balance: Unpaid principal on a loan.

Remaining Term: The time it will take to pay off the rest of an installment loans scheduled.

Remedies: The means of enforcing a right.

Renewal: The automatic re-establishment of in-force status affected by the payment of another premium.

Reorganization Plan: A Chapter 11 or 13 plan describing the terms by which the debtor intends to repay his/her debts, usually over a three to five-year period.

Repayment Plan: Modification of an existing loan after the borrower has been delinquent. Often used when the borrower misses' payments but the lender does not foreclose.

Replacement Cost: The dollar amount needed to replace damaged personal property or dwelling property without deducting for depreciation but limited by the maximum dollar amount shown on the declarations page of the policy.

Repossession: Seizure of assets used to secure a debt when the debt becomes delinquent.

Rescission: Withdrawal or cancellation.

Reserve: An amount representing actual or potential liabilities kept by an insurer to cover debts to policyholders. A reserve is usually treated as a liability.

Resident Alien: A person who is a legal permanent resident, but not a citizen, of the United States.

Residential Mortgage Transaction: Transaction with the lender whereby real property is given as collateral in exchange for funds.

Residual Benefit: In disability insurance, a benefit paid when you suffer a loss of income due to a covered disability or if loss of income persists. This benefit is based on a formula specified in your policy and it is generally a percentage of the full benefit. It may be paid up to the maximum benefit period.

Residual Value: The value of property at the end of a specific time period, especially at the end of a lease term.

Returned or "Bounced" Check Charge: Also referred to as an NSF or non-sufficient funds fee. The amount of money charged to an account holder whose account has insufficient funds available to pay the check, which is returned to the party who cashed it unpaid. (The bank did not advance the funds to cover check).

Return on Policyholder Surplus (Return on Equity): The sum of after-tax net income and unrealized capital gains, to the mean of prior and current year-end policyholder surplus, expressed as a percent. This ratio measures a company's overall after-tax profitability from underwriting and investment activity.

Revolver: A term credit card issuers use for card holders who roll over part of the bill to the next month, instead of paying off the balance in full each month. About seven out of ten cardholders revolve their debt.

Revolving Credit: A line of credit that does not have a specified repayment schedule but may require a minimum payment to cover interest and contribute to paying off principal. Typical of credit card loans, checking account cash reserve or overdraft accounts that have pre-approved lines of credit.

Revolving Line of Credit: An agreement to lend a specific amount to a borrower, and to allow that amount to be borrowed again once it has been repaid. Most credit cards offer revolving credit.

Right of Rescission: A provision of the federal Truth-in-Lending Act that allows a borrower to change his or her mind and cancel a loan within three days.

Right of Set-Off: Typically a lender's right to take money from a borrower's other accounts to pay for a specific debt owed that lender.

Risk Class: Risk class, in insurance underwriting, is a grouping of insureds with a similar level of risk. Typical underwriting classifications are preferred, standard and substandard, smoking and nonsmoking, male and female.

Risk Management: Management of the pure risks to which a company might be subject. It involves analyzing all exposures to the possibility of loss and determining how to handle these exposures through practices such as avoiding the risk, retaining the risk, reducing the risk, or transferring the risk, usually by insurance.

Risk Retention Groups: Liability insurance companies owned by their policyholders. Membership is limited to people in the same business or activity, which exposes them to similar liability risks. The purpose is to assume and spread liability exposure to group members and to provide an alternative risk financing mechanism for liability. These entities are formed under the Liability Risk Retention Act of 1986. Under law, risk retention groups are precluded from writing certain coverage's, most notably property lines and workers' compensation. They predominately write medical malpractice, general liability, professional liability, products liability and excess liability coverage's. They can be formed as a mutual or stock company, or a reciprocal.

Rule of 78s: Method of computing rebates of interest on installment loans. Its basis is the sum of the year's digits for determining the interest earned by the finance company for each month of a year, assuming equal monthly payments. It gets its name from the fact that the sum of the digits 1 through 12 is 78. Thus, interest is equal to 12/78ths of the total annual interest in the first month, 1l/78ths in the second month, and so on.

S&L Savings and Loan Association: A state or federally chartered depository financial institution that was primarily a provider of home mortgages but since deregulation in the 1980's to offer services similar to a commercial bank.

Savings and Loan Association: A state or federally chartered depository financial institution that was primarily a provider of home mortgages but since deregulation in the 1980's to offer services similar to a commercial bank.

Savings Bank: A type of depository financial institution, found mostly in the northeastern United States that accepts consumer deposits and invests these funds primarily in residential mortgages and high-grade securities. Mutual savings banks are owned by their depositors, while stock savings banks issue common stock to the public.

Schumer Box: The table of information about credit card rates and terms, named after Senator Chuck Schumer (D-NY), who was the author of it. It was part of the 1988 Truth-in-Lending Act (TILA) and dictates that every credit card solicitation must include it. It took effect in 2000. Credit card companies are required to list long term rates in at least 18-point type and all other rates, terms and conditions in at least 12-point type.

Secondary Market: The secondary market is populated by buyers willing to pay what they determine to be fair market value.

Section 1035 Exchange: This refers to a part of the Internal Revenue Code that allows owners to replace a life insurance or annuity policy without creating a taxable event.

Section 7702: Part of the Internal Revenue Code that defines the conditions a life policy must satisfy to qualify as a life insurance contract, which has tax advantages.

Secured: Protected (pledge of property to assure a creditor of payment).

Secured Card: A type of credit card that is linked to a bank account. A person's credit limit is based on how much money they have in their bank account. This card is ideal for people who have problems spending more than they can pay off.

Secured Credit Card: A secured credit card is one in which the financial institution issues a card with a maximum that is equal to a deposit that the cardholder puts down. These cards are a good choice for people trying to establish or rebuild credit.

Secured Debt: A debt that is secured by a lien on debtor's property that may be taken by the creditor in case of nonpayment by the debtor. A common example is a mortgage loan.

Secured Loan: Borrowed money that is backed by collateral.

Security: Property designated as collateral.

Security Freeze: Also known as a credit freeze, a security freeze is essentially a lockdown on your credit report and score. It blocks new lenders from accessing your credit file without your permission. Since most credit issuers require a credit check before granting credit, the security freeze should block most unauthorized attempts to obtain new credit in your name.

Security Interest: An interest in property given as collateral for a debt.

Separate Account: A separate account is an investment option that is maintained separately from an insurer's general account. Investment risk associated with separate-account investments is born by the contract owner.

Separate property: An individual's property that is not commingled with another's property.

Service Charge: Fees charged to customers for specific services or as a penalty for not meeting certain requirements such as insufficient funds in a checking account.

Settled Account: A customer has repaid their credit card balance.

Simple Interest: Interest computed only on the principal balance, without compounding.

Simple Interest Loan: A method of allocating the monthly payment between interest and principal. The

interest charged is determined by the unpaid principal balance on the loan, the interest rate, and the number of days since the last payment. The rest of the payment goes to the principal. Making early payments or additional payments will reduce the loan's principal and cut the total interest paid over the life of the loan.

Skimming: The act of copying one credit cards magnetic strip information onto a different credit card. If a person has purchases on their statement that they know they didn't make they should contact their credit card company immediately.

Smart Cards: A card that has a pre-determined limit of cash, which is then drawn off with every purchase. The card stores information on a microprocessor or memory chip rather than the magnetic stripe found on ATM and credit cards.

Solvency: Having sufficient assets-capital, surplus, reserves — and being able to satisfy financial requirements — investments, annual reports, examinations: to be eligible to transact insurance business and meet liabilities.

Standard Auto: Auto insurance for average drivers with relatively few accidents during lifetime.

Standard Card: The basic card offered by issuers. Customers with higher incomes and good credit reports can qualify for the higher-limit gold and platinum cards.

Standard Payment Calculation: A method of figuring out how many monthly payments there should be, based on the beginning loan balance, the term and the interest rate.

State of Domicile: The state in which the company is incorporated or chartered. The company also is licensed (admitted) under the state's insurance statutes for those lines of business for which it qualifies.

Statement: Shows your balance transfers, finance charges, interest rate, payments, purchases, and rewards for last month's billing cycle. A statement is usually mailed to a person every month.

Statutes: A written law that is passed by a governing authority, usually a state legislature or Congress.

Statute of Limitations: A statute stating the period of time in which a claim can be brought before a court.

Statutory Reserve: A reserve, either specific or general, required by law.

Stay: Act by the bankruptcy judge to stop all creditor action toward the debtor.

Stock Insurance Company: An incorporated insurer with capital contributed by stockholders, to whom earnings are distributed as dividends on their shares.

Stop Loss: Any provision in a policy designed to cut off an insurer's losses at a given point.

Subaccount Charge: The fee to manage a subaccount, which is an investment option in variable products that is separate from the general account.

Sub-Prime Borrower: A borrower with a less than perfect credit report due to late payments or a default on debt payments. Lenders often grade them based on the severity of past credit problems, with categories ranging from "A" to "D" or lower.

Sub-Prime Credit Card: A card offered to people with poor or severely poor credit history. They often carry very high interest rates, large annual fees and severe punitive fees. Usually, consumers are better off getting a secured credit card.

Subrogation: The right of an insurer who has taken over another's loss also to take over the other person's right to pursue remedies against a third party.

Subscriber: Customer of the credit bureaus who may request credit reports.

Successive Periods: In hospital income protection, when confinements in a hospital are due to the same or related causes and are separated by less than a contractually stipulated period of time, they are considered part of the same period of confinement.

Superior Claim: A claim against property, usually by a lender, that takes priority over another claim (i.e., that must be paid before another claim against the same property can be paid).

Surplus: The amount by which assets exceed liabilities.

Surrender Charge: Fee charged to a policyholder when a life insurance policy or annuity is surrendered for its cash value. This fee reflects expenses the insurance company incurs by placing the policy on its books, and subsequent administrative expenses.

Surrender Period: A set amount of time during which you have to keep the majority of your money in an annuity contract. Most surrender periods last from five to 10 years. Most contracts will allow you to take out at least 10% a year of the accumulated value of the account, even during the surrender period. If you take out more than that 10%, you will have to pay a surrender charge on the amount that you have withdrawn above that 10%.

T(tiered): If the letter T appears after the annual percentage rate (APR) on Bank rate rates table, the interest rate is based on tiered pricing, with different periodic rates applied to different levels of the outstanding balance. The rate shown applies to the lowest of the balance tiers.

Teaser Rate: Also called the introductory rate, this is the below market interest rate offered when a person first applies for a credit card.

Tenants by The Entireties: A manner of holding title to property by husband and wife, recognized in nearly one-third of all states, whereby each party holds title to the entire property, and it cannot be divided without the consent of both husband and wife.

Ten Year Treasury Constant Maturity: An index published by the Federal Reserve Board based on the average yield of a range of Treasury securities, all adjusted to the equivalent of a 10-year maturity. Yields on Treasury securities at constant maturity are determined by the U.S. Treasury from the daily yield curve. That is based on the closing market bid yields on actively traded Treasury securities in the over the counter market.

Term: The time to the maturity of a loan or deposit, expressed in months or years.

Term Life Insurance: Life insurance that provides protection for a specified period of time. Common policy periods are one year, five years, 10 years or until the insured reaches age 65 or 70. The policy doesn't build up any of the nonforfeiture values associated with whole life policies.

The Fed: Congress founded the Federal Reserve Board, the central bank of the United States, in 1913. It conducts the nation's monetary policy and regulates its banks in order to achieve a flexible and stable economy. The seven members of the Board of Governors of the Federal Reserve System are nominated by the President and confirmed by the Senate to serve 14-year terms. The chairman of the Board of Governors was Alan Greenspan. The chairman and the vice chairman of the board are named by the Senate. They serve a term of four years.

Thrift: A general term encompassing savings banks, savings and loan associations and credit unions.

Tort: A private wrong, independent of contract and committed against an individual, which gives rise to a legal liability and is adjudicated in a civil court. A tort can be either intentional or unintentional, and liability insurance is mainly purchased to cover unintentional torts.

Total Admitted Assets: This item is the sum of all admitted assets, and is valued in accordance with state laws and regulations, as reported by the company in its financial statements filed with state insurance regulatory authorities. This item is reported net as to encumbrances on real estate (the amount of any encumbrances on real estate is deducted from the value of the real estate) and net as to amounts recoverable from reinsurers (which are deducted from the corresponding liabilities for unpaid losses and unearned premiums).

Total Annual Loan Cost: The projected annual average coast of a reverse mortgage including all itemized costs.

Total Expense Ratio: The percentage of monthly debt payments compared to the total before tax income.

Total Loss: A loss of sufficient size that it can be said no value is left. The complete destruction of the property. The term also is used to mean a loss requiring the maximum amount a policy will pay.

Transaction: The act of purchasing an item, receiving a cash advance, transferring a balance, or making a payment. Your transactions are listed on your monthly statement.

Transaction Date: The date that goods or services were purchased or the date the cash advance was made.

TransUnion: National Credit Reporting Agency.

Treasury Index: A table of yields being paid on government debt, used to determine interest rate changes for adjustable rate mortgages and other variable rate loans.

Truth in Lending Act: A federal law that requires lenders to provide certain information so borrowers can compare one loan to another. The most important facts lenders must provide are: finance charges in dollars and as an annual percentage rate (APR), the credit issuer or company providing the credit line and the size of the credit line, length of grace period, if any, before payment must be made, minimum payment required, any annual fees and fees for credit insurance, if any.

Two Cycle Average Daily Balance: When figuring the interest on a credit card, the company will take the average of the last two billing cycles.

If a person has this on their credit card, they should switch cards, because you will pay a lot more in interest that a credit card that uses the average daily balance to figure the interest.

Two Cycle Billing: Means the same as Two Cycle Average Daily Balance. You should find a credit card that uses the average daily balance to calculate the interest. To find out which method your credit card company is using, you need to look at your statement, or your contract. If you still can't find it, you can call the company and they are required to tell you.

Two Year Treasury Constant Maturity: An index published by the Federal Reserve Board based on the average yield of a range of Treasury securities, all adjusted to the equivalent of a two-year maturity. Yields on Treasury securities at constant maturity are determined by the U.S. Treasury from the daily yield curve. That is based on the closing market-bid yields on actively traded Treasury securities in the over the counter market.

Umbrella Policy: Coverage for losses above the limit of an underlying policy or policies, such as homeowners and auto insurance. While it applies to losses over the dollar amount in the underlying policies, terms of coverage are sometimes broader than those of underlying policies.

Unaffiliated Investments: These investments represent total unaffiliated investments as reported in the exhibit of admitted assets. It is cash, bonds, stocks, mortgages, real estate and accrued interest, excluding investment in affiliates and real estate properties occupied by the company.

Underwriter: The individual trained in evaluating risks and determining rates and coverages for them. Also, an insurer.

Underwriting: The process of selecting risks for insurance and classifying them according to their degrees of insurability so that the appropriate rates may be assigned. The process also includes rejection of those risks that do not qualify.

Underwriting Expenses Incurred: Expenses, including net commissions, salaries and advertising costs, which are attributable to the production of net premiums written.

Underwriting Expense Ratio: This represents the percentage of a company's net premiums written that went toward underwriting expenses, such as commissions to agents and brokers, state and municipal taxed, salaries, employee benefits and other operating costs. The ration is computed by dividing underwriting expenses by net premiums written. A company with an underwriting expense ratio of 31.3% is spending more than 31 cents of every dollar of net premiums written to pay underwriting costs. It should be noted that different lines of business have intrinsically differing expense ratios. For example, boiler and machinery insurance, which requires a corps of skilled inspectors, is a high expense ratio line. On the other hand, expense ratios are usually low on group health insurance.

Underwriting Guide: Details the underwriting practices of an insurance company and provides specific guidance as to how underwriters should analyze all of the various types of applicants they might encounter. An Underwriting Guide is also called an underwriting manual, underwriting guidelines, or manual of underwriting policy.

Unearned Premiums: That part of the premium applicable to the unexpired part of the policy period.

Uninsured Motorist Coverage: Endorsement to a personal automobile policy that covers collision with a driver who does not have liability insurance.

Universal Life Insurance: A combination flexible premium, adjustable life insurance policy.

Unsecured: Unprotected; without security.

Unsecured Claim: A claim or debt for which a creditor holds no special assurance of payment, unlike a mortgage or lien; a debt for which credit was extended based solely upon the creditor's assessment of the debtor's future ability to pay.

Universal Default: A policy some lenders use to punish borrowers who pay any creditor late. It is most commonly used by credit card companies and revealed in the fine print of their contracts with consumers.

Unsecured Claim: A claim or debt for which a creditor holds no special assurance of payment, unlike a mortgage or lien, a debt for which credit was extended based solely upon the creditor's assessment of the debtor's future ability to pay.

Unsecured Debt: Debt that is not guaranteed by the pledge of any collateral. Most credit cards are unsecured debt, which is a main reason why their interest rate is higher than other forms of lending, such as mortgages, which employ property as collateral.

Unsecured Loan: An advance of money that is not secured by collateral.

Usage Data: Data regarding an individual's going, and how much time is spent at a specific site. This is particularly useful for advertisers, whose payments are based on how many times the Web page containing their advertisement is viewed. Also, online services such as America Online, who must track users sign on and sign off times for billing purposes.

Usual, Customary and Reasonable Fees: An amount customarily charged for or covered for similar services and supplies which are medically necessary, recommended by a doctor or required for treatment.

Usurious Rate: A rate based on unnecessarily or unlawfully high interest; act or practice of lending money at high interest; sometimes intangible property taxes are applied to income from usurious rates.

Usury: Illegal, excessive interest.

Utilization: How much a covered uses a particular health plan or program.

Valuation: A calculation of the policy reserve in life insurance. Also, a mathematical analysis of the financial condition of a pension plan.

Valuation Reserve: A reserve against the contingency that the valuation of assets, particularly investments, might be higher than what can be actually realized or that a liability may turn out to be greater than the valuation placed on it.

V (Variable): If the letter V appears after the annual percentage rate (APR) the interest rate is variable and subject to change.

Variable Annuitization: The act of converting a variable annuity from the accumulation phase to the payout phase.

Variable Interest Rate: The interest rate on a credit card that fluctuates based on the prime rate.

Variable Life Insurance: A form of life insurance whose face value fluctuates depending on the value of the dollar, securities or other equity products supporting the policy at the time payment is due.

Variable Rate: Annual percentage rate that periodically goes up or down, based on fluctuations in market interest rates as reflected in a published index (such as the prime rate published in the Wall Street Journal).

Variable Universal Life Insurance: A combination of the features of variable life insurance and universal life insurance under the same contract. Benefits are variable based on the value of underlying equity investments, and premiums and benefits are adjustable at the option of the policyholder.

Verification of Employment: Confirmation that a loan applicant is telling the truth about where he or she works and how much he or she makes.

Viatical Settlement Provider: Someone who serves as a sales agent, but does not actually purchase policies.

Viator: The terminally ill person who sells his or her life insurance policy.

VISA: VISA cards, a product of VISA USA, are distributed by financial institutions around the world. A VISA card holder borrows money against a credit line and repays those funds with interest if the balance is carried over from month to month in a revolving line of credit.

Void: To invalidate. When you void a check, you are canceling the check so no one can cash it. When you void a credit card transaction you are reversing the transaction.

Voluntary Reserve: An allocation of surplus not required by law. Insurers often accumulate such reserves to strengthen their financial structure.

Waiting Period: See "elimination period".

Waiver: The intentional and voluntary giving up of rights or claims.

Waiver of Premium: A provision in some insurance contracts which enable an insurance company to waive the collection of premiums while keeping the policy in force if the policyholder becomes unable to work because of an accident or injury. The waiver or premium for disability remains in effect as long as the ensured is disabled.

Wall Street Journal Prime Rate: The Wall Street Journal surveys large banks and publishes the consensus prime rate. It's the most widely quoted measure of the prime rate, which a common benchmark for consumer and business loans is set by banks, often at a level 3 percentage points higher than the federal funds rate. The prime rate will move up or down in lock step with changes by the Federal Reserve Board.

Whole Life Insurance: Life insurance which might be kept in force for a person's whole life and which pays a benefit upon the person's death, whenever that might be.

Willfully: Intentionally.

Writ: A legal document ordering an authorized person to do a certain act (or to refrain from doing something).

Write-Off-Action taken by a creditor to consider a debt uncollectable, thereby taking a loss for tax purposes.

WSJ Prime Rate: The initials stand for the Wall Street Journal, which surveys large banks and publishes the consensus prime rate. It's the most widely quoted measure of the prime rate, which a common benchmark for consumer and business loans is set by banks, often at a level 3 percentage points higher than the federal funds rate. The prime rate will move up or down in lock step with changes by the Federal Reserve Board.

Yield on Invested Assets (IRIS): Annual net investment income after expenses, divided by the mean of cash and net invested assets. This ratio measures the average return on a company's invested assets. This ratio is before capital gains/losses and income taxes.

Zero Balance: When a credit card customer's bill has been paid off and there are no new charges during that billing cycle.

RESOURCES

This section of the book has a list of resources that will be helpful when seeking help to solve some credit issues. I realize that many people will never pay attention to this section of the book, but you should because these resources can help you with your fight to clean your credit. Remember to use these resources as a research tool. There is always someone out there that will give you a piece of information that you can use as a weapon.

Advanced Resolution Services Inc.
5005 Rockside Road
Suite 600
Independence, OH. 44131
1-800-392-8911
1-216-615-7642 (fax)

SageStream LLC Consumer Office
P.O. Box 503793
San Diego, CA. 92150
1-888-395-0277
www.sagestreamllc.com

LexisNexis Consumer Center
P.O. Box 105108
Atlanta, Georgia 30348-5108
1-888-497-0011
1-866-868-9534
1-800-456-1244

LexisNexis Risk Solutions Bureau LLC
Consumer Center
Attention: Banko
P.O. Box 105108
Atlanta, GA. 30348-5108

Problem-Resolution Resources
Council of Better Business Bureaus
4200 Wilson Blvd., Suite 800
Arlington, VA 22203
www.bbb.org
703-276-0100

Credit Bureau Contact Information

Equifax Mailing Address
Equifax Credit Information Services, LLC
P.O. Box 740241, Atlanta, GA 30374

Equifax Phone Numbers:
866-349-5186: Dispute Credit Report Items
800-685-1111: Request Free Credit Report
888-766-0008: Place Fraud Alert on Profile
866-493-9788: Existing Customer Support
888-202-4025: Business Solutions
404-885-8078: Fax Number

Experian Mailing Address
Experian National Consumer Assistance Center
P.O. Box 4500, Allen, TX 75013
Experian Phone Numbers:
800-509-8495: Dispute Credit Report Items
888-397-3742: Report Requests & Fraud Help

877-284-7942: Existing Customer Support
888-243-6951: Business Credit Services
972-390-4908: Fax Line

TransUnion Mailing Address
TransUnion Consumer Relations
P.O. Box 2000, Chester, PA 19016-2000
TransUnion Phone Numbers:
800-916-8800: Disputes Items & Status Checks
877-322-8228: Free Annual Credit Report
800-888-4213: Purchase Credit Report
888-909-8872: Place a Security Freeze
800-493-2392: Credit Monitoring Customer Support
866-922-2100: Business Services Assistance
610-546-4771: Fax Machine

Innovis
Attn: Consumer Assistance
P.O. Box 1689
Pittsburgh, PA 15230-1689
(800) 540-2505
www.innovis.com
For Innovis corporate headquarters, contact:
Innovis
250 E. Town St.
Columbus, Ohio 43215

Contact Information for PRBC Inc.
(Payment Reporting Builds Credit)

A fifth credit reporting company is PRBC Inc., which performs the same functions as the other CRCs. However, it also allows consumers to build reports and a positive credit history using alternative data, such as timely bill, utility, and insurance payments. PRBC Inc. uses information not always reported to the other bureaus, allowing consumers to rebuild a positive credit history. The company is owned by MicroBilt Corporation.

MicroBilt Corporation
1640 Airport Rd, Suite 115
Kennesaw, GA 30144
(800) 884-4747
www.microbilt.com

Additional Mailing Address for credit bureaus.
TransUnion
P.O. Box 6790
Fullerton, CA 92834

Experian
P.O. Box 9530
Allen, TX 75013

Experian
P.O. Box 9532
Allen, TX. 75013

Experian
P.O. Box 4500
Allen, TX. 75013
Equifax
P.O. Box 740241
Atlanta, GA 30374

CSC Credit Services
P.O. Box 619054
Dallas, TX. 75261-9054

Telephone numbers to order your paper credit report from the three major credit bureaus.
Equifax: 1-800-685-1111
Experian: 1-888-397-3742
TransUnion: 1-800-888-4213

Addresses for three major credit bureaus fraud departments.
TransUnion
Fraud Victim Assistance Department
P.O. Box 6790
Fullerton, CA. 92634-6790

TransUnion
Fraud Department
P.O. Box 34012
Fullerton, CA. 92834

Equifax
Consumer Fraud Division
P.O. Box 740241
Atlanta, GA. 30374-0241

Equifax
Fraud Assistance
P.O. Box 105069
Atlanta, GA. 30348
1-404-885-8000
1-800-525-6285
Fax: 1-770-375-2821

Experian
National Consumer Assistance
P.O. Box 2104
Allen, TX. 75013
1-888-397-3742

Experian
P.O. Box
Allen, TX. 75013

To report the fraudulent use of your checks:
Check Rite
Phone: 800-766-2748

Chex Systems
Phone: 800-328-5121

CrossCheck
Phone: 800 552-1900

Equifax-Telecredit
Phone: 800-437-5120

NPC
Phone: 800-526-5380

SCAN
Phone: 800-262-7771

Tele-Check
Phone: 800 366-2425

REMOVE YOUR NAME FROM PRE-APPROVED CREDIT LISTS?

Call: (888) 5OPTOUT (888-567-8688)

Removes your name from pre-approved credit lists compiled by Equifax, Experian, and Trans Union.

REMOVE YOUR NAME FROM DIRECT MAIL LISTS?

E-mail: www.the-dma.org
Write: Direct Marketing Association
Mail Preference Service
P.O. Box 643
Carmel, NY 10512

REMOVE YOUR NAME FROM TELEPHONE LISTS?

E-mail: www.the-dma.org
Write: Direct Marketing Association
Telephone Preference Service
P.O. Box 1559
Carmel, NY 10512

REMOVE YOUR NAME FROM E-MAIL LISTS?

E-mail: www.e-mps.org

Professional association of elected state attorneys general. This site provides links to each state's website, where you can find consumer protection information specific to your state.

Federal Trade Commission (FTC)
CRC 240
Washington, DC 20580
www.ftc.gov
877-382-4357

Government agency that supervises the activities of credit bureaus, repair clinics, and collection agencies.

FTC'S Identity Theft Hotline

www.consumer.gov/idtheft

1-877-IDTHEFT (1-877-438-4338)

Hotline charged with collecting complaints about identity theft at its regional offices. They also can provide an Identity Theft Affidavit that you can submit to your creditors.

Information and Education Resources

This section will provide you with agencies that provide information and education in regards to your credit as well as debt.

Consumer Information Center

Pueblo, CO 81009

www.pueblo.gsa.gov

1-800-FED-INFO (1-800-333-4636)

Federal government central distribution center for consumer information.

Membership organization that promotes ethical business practices. It provides referrals to the local office that serves the area where the company you are doing business with is located. It can help to resolve issues evolving from identity theft.

National Association of Attorneys General (NAAG)

750 First St. NE, Suite 1100

Washington, DC 20002

www.naag.org

202-326-6000